Index

Contributors

The following people, successful professionals in their respective fields of expertise, are here to help us on our parenting journey by embracing the challenge that is raising multicultural children.

Elisavet Arkolaki is the curator of this guide and author of the children's book 'Where am I from?'. Passionate about travel and inspired by global learning, she raises her own children in between countries, cultures, and languages. She writes to build cultural understanding and sensitivity in young children while they are still eager to learn. She graduated from the University of Liverpool with a degree in Global Marketing (MSc), the University of Athens with a degree in French Language and Literature (BSc), and was awarded a certificate of proficiency in English from the University of Cambridge.

Website: www.maltamum.com
Facebook: Maltamum, Elisavet Arkolaki's Behind The Book Club
Email: liza@maltamum.com

Dr. Ute Limacher-Riebold is an independent Intercultural Language Consultant with a passion and love for languages. As a multilingual linguist, she works with families who speak multiple languages at home. She supports them in maintaining their heritage languages and cultures, and in finding a healthy balance with all the languages and cultures they collect during their international journey. With her personalized Family Language Plan© they can design their own multilingual journey, and define short and long term language goals for the whole family. She is a life-long international and ATCK (Adult Third Culture Kid), and raises her own three children as multilinguals and multiculturals, abroad too. She translates research into evidence-based, easy to apply tips for parents, families and practitioners to use in everyday life. She holds workshops on raising multilingual children successfully and other topics related to international life. She has lived and worked in Italy, Switzerland, France and the Netherlands and is fluent in Italian, German, French, English, Dutch and Swiss-German.

Website: www.UtesInternationalLounge.com
Twitter: utesintlounge
Youtube: Ute's International Lounge
Facebook page: UtesInternationalLounge
Facebook group: Multilingual Families

Vivian Chiona holds a Bachelor's degree in Psychology, as well as Master's degrees in both Child & Adolescent Psychology and Health Psychology, and a further specialization in Intercultural Psychology and online work – all of which led to Expat Nest. She is a bi-cultural, multilingual expat with family all over the world, and she is well familiar with the blessings of a mobile life but she is also well aware of its challenges. Vivian has successfully consulted with more than 1000 clients and has delivered training on a variety of topics, such as transition, Third Culture Kids (TCKs), coping with change, dealing with stress, bereavement, and expat loss, violence prevention, special educational needs and inclusion, and understanding diversity - to name but a few.

Website: www.expatnest.com
Facebook page: ExpatNest
LinkedIn: Vivian Chiona

Dr. Brigitte Vittrup is a professor of child development at Texas Woman's University. She holds a Ph.D. in Developmental Psychology from The University of Texas at Austin, and her research focuses on parent socialization practices, children's racial attitudes, and media influences on children. Brigitte was born and raised in Denmark and is currently living and raising her children in the USA.

Website: Texas Woman's University

Brian Vassallo is the Assistant Head of School at Mariam Albatool School and a visiting lecturer at the University of Malta. He is a graduate in Psychology and in Inclusive Education from the University of Malta and a Master's graduate in Educational Leadership from the University of Leicester UK. He is the author of numerous research papers and his research interests include Multicultural Educational Leadership, Cultural and Disability Inclusion.

Email: brianvassallo7671@gmail.com

Rita Rosenback is a Family Language Coach, speaker, and author. Her book "Bringing up a Bilingual Child" is an easy-to-read guide navigating readers across the "Seven Cs of Multilingual Parenting: Communication, Confidence, Commitment, Consistency, Creativity, Culture and Celebration". She also works as an Intercultural Youth Trainer, she is on the board of 'Multicultural Kid Blogs' and has served for several years as the Vice President of 'FIGT - Families in Global Transition'. Rita offers individual family language coaching, including tailor-made Family Language Plans. She was born a Finland-Swede, and after stays in Germany and in India, she now lives in the UK. She has two multilingual adult daughters and is currently helping to pass on Swedish to her grandsons.

Website: www.multilingualparenting.com
Facebook page: Multilingual Parenting (frequent free live QA sessions on multilingualism)
Facebook group: Multilingual Parenting
Email: rita.rosenback@multilingualparenting.com

Dr. Mary-Pat O'Malley-Keighran is a Speech & Language Therapist with over 20 years of experience working with children & their families. She is a lecturer in speech and language therapy at NUI Galway and she is passionate about supporting multilingual families to develop all of their child's languages while still having fun!

Website: www.www.talknua.com
Facebook page: Talk Nua

Tamara Yousry is an Anglo-Egyptian -and Third Culture Kid- who has lived in several countries including Kuwait, Egypt, England, Scotland, Norway, Singapore, and Australia. She has a Bachelor's degree with a major in Journalism and Mass Communications and a minor in Psychology from The American University in Cairo, and a Master of Arts degree in Intercultural Communication from The University of Bedfordshire in the UK.

Email: tamarasyousry@gmail.com
Instagram: ytamara1234

Lisa Ferland is raising bilingual children in Sweden after moving from the USA in 2012. She has academic training in public health epidemiology. Over 10 years of experience in project management, data analysis, and global public health capacity building, meant that she was already globally-minded, detail-oriented, and open to new challenges before she took the plunge and moved abroad with her husband. She is the editor of the "Knocked Up Abroad" anthologies and writer of the children's book series "When the Clock Strikes".

Website: www.knockedupabroad.com
Facebook: knockedupabroad

Yui Mikuriya is a 17-year-old Japanese girl who now lives in Tokyo. Living across three countries, she has never felt accepted as part of a specific culture and has always struggled with her sense of identity. Despite the existence of the Third Culture Kids community, she felt there was something missing, and therefore decided to come up with a new inclusive ideology for multicultural kids and others, the Bridging Kids.

Email: yui.mikuriya@gmail.com
Facebook: Yui Mikuriya

Quotes and advice from the following people have been used in the third and fifth chapters.

Irene Bloemraad, Ph.D., is an Associate Professor in Sociology, and the Thomas Garden Barnes Chair of Canadian Studies at the University of California, Berkeley, as well as a Scholar with the Canadian Institute for Advanced Research.

Chontelle Bonfiglio is a certified ESL teacher, writer, and mother of two bilingual kids. She offers practical advice for parents seeking to raise bilingual or multilingual children; with inspiration, support and strategies based on her experience as a parent, and as a teacher of a foreign language to children.

Marianna Pogosyan, Ph.D., is an intercultural consultant specializing in the psychology of cross-cultural transitions. Intercultural consultant and author of Psychology Today's Between Cultures.

Erin N. Winkler is an associate professor of Africology and Urban Studies at the University of Wisconsin-Milwaukee, where she has also served on the advisory boards of Childhood and Adolescent Studies; Ethnic Studies; and Latin American, Caribbean, and US Latin Studies; and is affiliated faculty in Women's Studies.

Reid Lyon, Ph.D., former Chief of the Child Development and Behavior Branch within the National Institute of Child Health and Human Development (NICHD) at the National Institute of Health (NIH) in the USA.

Annabelle Humanes, Ph.D., background lies in applied linguistics, bilingualism and second language acquisition. She has a Ph.D. in Bilingual Language Acquisition. She wrote a 300-page thesis on children acquiring two languages (French and English) from birth. She looked in particular at the development of their vocabulary from the time they started talking to around their 3rd birthday.

TED talk titled 'Where is Home' by writer **Pico Iyer**, who himself has three or four "origins". He meditates on the meaning of home, the joy of traveling and the serenity of standing still. He contemplates the idea that home has more to do with a piece of your soul rather than soil.

TED talk titled 'Multiculturalism as a threat and multiculturalism as an asset' by the Canadian Ph.D. student of Kurdish origin, Rébar Jaff. He talks about his life experiences as a child refugee who was then welcomed as a first-class citizen in Canada, and how this positive experience and sense of belonging propelled him forward towards a creative life journey.

Another inspirational TED talk that poses lots of questions, and challenges our perception of how and why things are in certain ways, is 'Don't ask where I'm from, ask where I'm a local' by writer **Taiye Selasi**.

Inventing identities for our multicultural children

by Elisavet Arkolaki

Intercultural and interracial marriages are on the rise according to studies, whilst more parents, particularly in the USA and Europe, are adopting children from other countries. As a result, our communities are growing increasingly diverse and it is no longer surprising to see families composed of different ethnicities and cultures.

My family is an example of this. Our kids were born in different countries and have different nationalities. The eldest, Erik, has lived in four countries, speaks three languages and understands four. He can't identify 100% with any one country he has lived in. According to the United Nations Population Fund (2015), he is just one of 244 million people recorded to be living outside their country of origin.

I, on the other hand, have lived in six countries and speak three languages fluently. My husband, who is from a different country of origin than mine, also speaks three languages and has traveled all over the world. The biggest advantages that I see in a mixed cultural background and global mobility, besides the benefit of language comprehension which I address in my blog post 'Our Journey with Raising Multilingual Children' on maltamum.com, is the opportunity this allows for learning to see the world from different perspectives. Being immersed in different cultures encourages the development of character traits such as adaptability, compassion, and tolerance.

Rita Rosenback stated that "All my languages are an intrinsic part of my identity. Every single one of them has helped me understand other people and cultures and thus contributed to the person I am today. They do however not split my identity, they consolidate it."

I love this quote and I feel the same way, too. I appreciate how we as adults are able to take this optimistic perspective. But for a child, the reality of being multilingual and multicultural may be interpreted in a less favorable way and they need our guidance to get there. Identity is very closely knitted with culture. When the cultures are so blended and the background so fluid, our children need our help to invent a positive identity of their own; an identity that is not defined by one sole culture.

In order to build a strong identity and a confident sense of self, our children need to feel proud of their cultural background. They also need to learn how to be open and accepting towards whatever culture they now find themselves in which through integration will inevitably come to shape their identity too.

Children don't really start to ponder over identity issues until later in life but the roots of many of these are to be found in early childhood. My books help to create a foundation of normalcy and acceptance for our multicultural children during their early years.

'Where am I from?' is a story that will resonate with our preschoolers and early readers. Through stunning murals, painted on the walls of public primary schools by artist Platon, this book will take children to a quest in search of common origins. A most appealing story for kids of mixed heritage as they are the ones usually at a loss when asked to answer where they are from.

Our initiative received lots of support from our global community. I am proud to say that this project got fully funded on Kickstarter in August 2018 and we raised about 12,500 USD within 30 days to create "Where am I from?". We received funding in the form of pre-orders from many generous individuals, and three public sector institutions in Norway and Malta. During the campaign, we got press coverage in three countries, and our efforts have been featured in several blogs and websites worldwide. All the book characters are based on real people who all except one are of mixed heritage. The book is published by Faraxa Publishing and can also be purchased on Amazon.

'How to Raise Confident Multicultural Children', the book you are currently reading, is a resource guide for the parent and the teacher, as a way to pay it forward, and give something to the global parenting community on which I rely for the future of my children, and of all the children of the world.

If you'd like to get in touch, I'd love to hear from you. My email is
liza@maltamum.com

Thank you for reading!

The debate over multiculturalism and what we can learn from the Canadian model

by Elisavet Arkolaki

With country leaders openly opposing multiculturalism, using claims that it undermines social cohesion and local cultural values, many people are wondering whether this holds true. Questions like the following are not uncommon. Does the acceptance of multiculturalism pose a threat to integration? Is it realistic to expect a thriving, unified community when we adhere to positive public acknowledgment, full acceptance, and tolerance of the ethnic, cultural and religious differences?

From an academic perspective, the following three-part definition of multiculturalism is presented in – George Crowder, Theories of Multiculturalism: an Introduction, Polity Press, 2013.

1. Multiculturalism starts with the observation that most contemporary societies are 'multicultural' – that is, they do in fact contain multiple cultures.
2. More distinctively, multiculturalists respond to that fact as something to approve of rather than opposing or merely tolerating.

3. More distinctively still, multiculturalists argue that the multiplicity of cultures within a single society should be not only generally approved of but also given positive recognition in the public policy and public institutions of the society.

Multiculturalism has many faces. We have Demographic Multiculturalism, Multiculturalism as Political Philosophy and Multiculturalism as Public Policy. These faces can vary greatly from one country to another. Different people, minority and majority groups perceive and translate the concepts and policies very differently. In this chapter, I would like us to look into the Canadian model, the country's thriving multi-colored communities and its citizens who first and foremost identify themselves as Canadian citizens.

Irene Bloemraad, Associate Professor in Sociology and the Thomas Garden Barnes Chair of Canadian Studies at the University of California, Berkeley, as well as a Scholar with the Canadian Institute for Advanced Research, gave an insightful short speech titled 'Why is Multiculturalism a Dirty Word in Europe?'. According to Bloemraad, part of this stems from the fact that for many Europeans multiculturalism as a concept is perceived as parallel societies that don't interact, and that's not the Canadian vision.

European politicians have been openly expressing opinions against multiculturalism; the German Chancellor Angela Merkel who infamously stated back in 2010 that multiculturalism has "utterly failed"; the former president of France, Nicolas Sarkozy; David Cameron in the UK; and many more. What is quite different between Canada and Europe is that in the former, leaders at the very highest echelons talk about multiculturalism in a positive way, and that sets the tone for society at large, and for political discourse.

How could things change? Bloemraad suggests that we should start by accepting the fact that immigrants in Europe are not going to disappear tomorrow, that their children are going to be born and to grow up in Europe, and that we have to reimagine European societies in a way that is more inclusive. The transformation can start by making drastic changes to our educational systems; change the way history and social studies are taught. This is what they did in Canada. Instead of presenting one voice that gives a homogenous history of the country, they have multiple voices from different backgrounds, presenting different perspectives on history.

Bloemraad concludes that ultimately, the way we see multiculturalism is a moral choice. If we acknowledge that immigrants are here to stay and we believe they have a legitimate right to stay in our country, then we need to find ways to include them. One way of doing that is by granting them full membership, citizenship or just even social inclusion. The research evidence clearly shows that multiculturalism and pluralism policy helps to make that inclusion possible.

A good example of such evidence is to be found in one of my favorite TEDx videos on the subject. A personal story and one which allows us to bring the spotlight on the human element behind the theories, the talk is that of the Canadian Ph.D. student of Kurdish origin, Rébar Jaff. He talks about his life experiences as a child refugee who was then welcomed as a first-class citizen in Canada, and how this positive experience and sense of belonging propelled him forward towards a creative life journey. Among other things, Jaff discusses the interesting way in which multiculturalism in Iraq is often viewed as a threat by its diverse ethnic groups while in contrast a much-richer multiculturalism in Canada is seen as one of the country's greatest assets.

Furthermore, in a similar vein, Bloemraad considered such diversity when she gave another very interesting speech titled 'You Are Your Citizenship'. She states the question 'Who are you?' can be answered as 'You are your citizenship'. In her own words "If you ask Canadians their sense of belonging and their pride in a Canadian identity and in being Canadian, nine out of ten roughly residents of Canada say that they feel like they belong to Canada and they're proud of being Canadian or a resident of Canada." which is quite an accomplishment. In this video, she gives the background story to that statement. In her paper 'The Debate Over Multiculturalism: Philosophy, Politics, and Policy', which deserves to be read in full, she asks a very valid question: "Does the promotion of pluralism and diversity conflict with social cohesion and immigrant integration, or is multiculturalism a pathway to incorporation?". Research findings demonstrate that "Immigrants living in countries that adopt multicultural policies are more likely to engage in nonviolent political activities directed at their country of residence rather than their homeland, more likely to report trust in government, less likely to report discrimination based on their group membership, and more likely to become citizens."

In Canada, Official Multiculturalism was introduced as a key policy in 1971. The Prime Minister Pierre Elliott Trudeau announced in his speech that the government would support minority communities, given that "National unity, if it is to mean anything in the deeply personal sense, must be founded on confidence in one's own individual identity." Central to this policy was the official recognition of the diverse cultures in a plural society, embedded in official French-English bilingualism, aiming for integration through intercultural exchange.

Nowadays, a policy governing multiculturalism is there to ensure that all citizens keep their identities, take pride in their ancestry, and have a sense of belonging. They hold celebrations in the different communities in order to appreciate the wealth and diversity of their society. But, above all, they identify themselves as Canadians. They have strong roots spread around the globe while at the same time they're flourishing in the land they call home.

Tamara Yousry noted in her chapter in this guide titled 'Crossing the Deep Cultural Divide' that "monocultural groups and teams are becoming a thing of the past. In today's contemporary, globalized world, multicultural groups are the norm." People will keep on crossing borders, falling in love, having children, and we need to learn how to coexist with each other in a respectful and caring manner. Instead of looking at countries where integration is failing us and where the blame for that is put on multiculturalism, we can look up to others who are succeeding and learn from them. Could Canada be the key?

My identity crisis growing up in numerous cultures

by Yui Mikuriya

My name, Yui, means "to connect" in Japanese, so perhaps because of that, I have always wanted to help connect people and bring cultures together. Have you ever heard of "third culture kids?" Well, that is exactly what I am. Let me tell you my story.

I was born in Japan. I loved going to school with my friends, and I thought this life would continue forever. But I was wrong. I was 7 when my parents decided to move to another country; France; and took me with them. I was too little to understand where France was, and I was amazed by the fact that my home country was not the only one in the world. I remember feeling afraid of going to a new place where I did not know anybody, not to mention my lack of language ability. My parents decided to put me in a local French school, where I had no way of communicating with any of my classmates. It didn't help that we lived in the countryside. I was the only Asian at school and my family was the only Asian family in town.

However, I adapted quickly to my new environment. I was able to enjoy elementary school and slowly stopped feeling homesick. But life never got easy. I'll never forget for instance my 8th birthday. My views on what I assumed to be universal societal norms were about to be challenged forever. I remember having to put on a brave face and ask my French friends to take off their shoes before they entered the house. This is the norm in Japanese culture, but my friends weren't accustomed to doing so. However, my friends were not the only ones who had a hard time accepting another culture; I was just the same. When it was my turn to go to my friend's birthday party, I was horrified to find her dad taking a nap on his bed with his shoes on.

I continued encountering harsh struggles.

As I walked down the street, older students from my school would yell out, calling me Chinese. I didn't really understand it at first, so it was okay. As I grew older, I heard it more and more, but I never got used to people identifying me as "Chinese" or "Asian". It felt like they were casting me out of their culture. I was an outsider, and I wasn't welcome in their world.

I wanted to get rid of the features that made me look Asian. Maybe having blue eyes and blond hair like my friends could make me a member of the inner circle. But appearances cannot be changed that easily.

So, I worked very hard to soak myself in South-Western French culture despite my looks. And I did! My behavior became very localized. People often commented on how my French had a strong South-West accent. But no matter how hard I tried, I never seemed to perfectly fit in. This constant mental dilemma has been spinning in my mind throughout my childhood.

Eventually, I proudly proclaimed myself as Japanese. This provided me with a comfort zone and protected me. But even though I embraced my Japanese heritage, my desire to assimilate into the French culture kept on growing bigger and bigger, occupying more and more space in my cultural identity. I slowly started losing my inherited Japanese self and I suffered a serious identity crisis.

This is why, after "living abroad" for 10 years, I decided to come back to Japan. I thought that I could finally live a simpler life being a part of just one culture where I belong. At long last, I could escape from being a third culture kid and be "normal". But I was wrong again. People didn't accept me as Japanese here anymore. In the place that I had always believed to be my true home, people considered me an outsider. There was no place for me where I could perfectly fit in. I realized that no matter where I go, I will always be considered as someone who doesn't really belong.

If so, why not celebrate me in all my third culture kid glory?

When we look at a glass filled halfway through with water, some will see it as half empty whereas others will see it as half full. This realization was the turning point in my way of thinking, and it helped me redefine my sense of self. I realized that I was not half empty. Rather, I am half full! And I possess two of these half-full glasses, a French and a Japanese one, each filled with its own blend of colors! Despite having all these identity crises, I am now able to establish my very own identity. I no longer feel that I have to choose one over the other. I am French, and I am also Japanese.

So, at that point in life, I knew I had to do something that was unique to me and my experiences. My contribution to this society was a service project called the "Hokusai Ambassador Project", which I started alongside the Sumida Hokusai Museum in Tokyo to accommodate French visitors. Hokusai is arguably the most famous Japanese artist from the 19th century, who has inspired Monet, Van Gogh and many more, as well as me. The first time I visited the Sumida Hokusai Museum, I heard many people speaking French, which reminded me of the popularity of Hokusai and Japanese culture in France. So, out of curiosity, I asked the staff about which foreigners most frequently visited, and I was told French.

Much to my surprise, the exhibition contents were only in Japanese, English, Chinese, and Korean, even though French people were the most common visitors. I asked the museum why this was the case, and why even the translations in English were lacking detailed information, let alone the absence of French. I received no proper feedback and it seemed that a basic literal translation was all that could be provided due to a lack of cultural understanding as well as affordability in the translation industry. I was met with a problem directly staring me in the face that only someone like myself, with profound understanding of both French and Japanese cultures, would be able to solve it. I decided that I wanted to make a change to help visitors striving to learn more about the culture of my home country, Japan. In this case, it was French, due to my language ability and my strong connection with France.

Moreover, I was invited in 2019 to talk about my challenges in a TEDx speech, titled 'Third culture kid? NO, no, no! Bridging Kids'. I introduced this new term, bridging kids, to describe TCKs under a new light that focuses on our capabilities. It's an inclusive term for millions of kids out there who like me are the melting pots of more than one culture. We are the Bridging Kids. Children who will, later on, turn into adults who can bridge gaps between cultures, adults who will be capable of feeling at home everywhere. Now, thanks to this new way of thinking, I am able to confidently step out in this world as a Bridging Kid and serve to create bridges in this divided society. I also hope to make bridges for others to follow in. In the future, I see myself using this skill of Bridging, to not only bridge cultures and people, but to bridge different fields of studies, such as Physics and Politics, two subjects I am currently interested in.

Chances are that you, the reader, are a TCK and/or you are raising a kid amongst cultures. Please cherish the moment of realization that the "lack of belonging" kids like us might feel growing up in a multicultural environment, become an element of our complete identity later on in life and an anchor to the whole wide world. What we feel like we're missing out in our early years, later on, becomes the essence of our identity.

If you also have a kid who struggles in life with their different cultures, please remind them of the unique opportunities that come hand in hand with the adversities. Embracing all the cultures that belong to her, will in time enable her to take action and bridge cultures. Bridging cultures can eventually help change our world for the better.

Why urging our children to embrace different cultures and learn different languages matters

by Dr. Ute Limacher-Riebold

Like many others who were born in one country, brought up in another (or more) and then moved to other places, I used to struggle when people asked me where I am from or where my home is. As a child, I wondered why people would ask me which country I like most, Germany or Italy, or which language I prefer, German or Italian. I learned to give the answer that was expected from me and that made others happy: my parents, my family, my friends. What I only discovered much later in life was that I wasn't the only person having a hard time to deal with these questions. Children who grow up outside of their countries of origin, or out of their parents' passport countries, actually have a name; Third Culture Kids (or Cross-Cultural Kids, etc.).

All of these children face more or less the same challenges. According to the latest definition of TCKs from Michael Pollock (3rd edition of "Third Culture Kids: Growing up among worlds", 2017), "A traditional third culture kid (TCK) is a person who spends a significant part of his or her first eighteen developmental years of life accompanying parent(s) into a country (or countries) different from at least one parent's passport country(ies) due to a parent's choice of work or advanced training".

I was born in Switzerland while my German parents were living just across the Italian border. I grew up in Lombardy (Italy) and moved to Switzerland for studies when I was 18. My parents left Germany in 1957 and after living in Belgium, moved to Italy for my father's work for a European organization. My sister and I didn't have a highly mobile childhood, but a childhood spent in different cultures: our parents'(German), the local (Italian), and the highly international one that we had the chance to immerse into at school, and in the community, we grew up in: our "third" culture.

I grew up knowing that as "guests in the country" (how our mother would explain our status as foreigners) we'd better adjust to the host culture in order to fully embrace our life there. My mother was a perfect example of how to do this: she taught herself Italian and was one of the few foreign spouses who preferred the connection with locals to the expat bubble. She would always see the positive side of everything. There were only a few situations that made me realize that the way we were living was not that common.

I never understood why others would call us "Germans" or foreigners in Italy and "Italians" or, again, foreigners in Germany. This being "neither... nor..." wasn't a problem for me. I understood very early that only people who were not in our situation would ask these questions out of curiosity and because they wanted to know how a child perceived this kind of life.

For me, speaking German at home and Italian with my friends was normal, and although many of my local friends spoke the local language only, I never really thought that speaking three languages at age 6 was "strange". Even though I saw that they would meet with their extended family regularly on the weekends and for special occasions, I never missed my extended family. I guess that if you don't know something you don't miss it.

It was only later when I was a teenager that I started comparing my life to the ones of my peers in Germany and Italy. I wondered how life would have been if my grandmother would have cooked for me as she did for my cousins, what my birthdays would have been if my extended family would have been present. But again, it wasn't a sad thought, it was one of curiosity. I didn't long for a life more like theirs, I was simply curious to know what my life would have been should my parents have stayed in Germany.

It was at age 14, when I spent a few weeks with my aunts and grandparents alone in Germany, that I discovered my "Germanness". I got a feeling for what life in Germany could be. I spent a lot of time with my cousins who happened to be my peers. I did my best to fit in, to belong to the groups I was hanging out with. I listened to their music, used the same language and slang, and started understanding their jokes. For the first time in my life, I felt what it would be like living in a place where everyone speaks my home language. But I also felt sad because I had to hide my Italian-self as nobody spoke Italian or knew about Italian culture.

Growing up as a German in Italy in the 70s/80s was not always a pleasure. When I was 8 a young child was forbidden to play with me because I was German – his grandfather died in WWII and the family resented all Germans for this loss. When Italy played against Germany at the FIFA world cup, my father hid our car with the German number plate in the garage, out of fear that someone would damage it. As a teenager, I avoided telling new friends that I'm German in order to fit in. I didn't want to attract attention or be compared to the German tourists that would come to our town.

The desire to fit in and feel a sense of belonging in a group of friends is very natural and healthy. It means that we want to fully embrace the otherness. The same way I switched from one language to another, I switched my behavior and the way I presented myself from German to Italian, to my original Italo-German. It was my way to adapt with innate flexibility to different situations and settings. This kind of switching is very common among adaptable people, and it seems to be one of the many advantages of children who grow up between different cultures.

When I was 18 years old, I moved to Switzerland to study at the University of Zurich and learned to find my way in a new culture without my parents. I learned the importance of punctuality and that one can have dinner at 6 pm, among other things.

Although I enrolled in Romanistics, I studied several semesters of Germanistics, Psychology, English, and Journalism, just because I was fascinated by these topics. I obtained my University degree in Italian and French Literature and Linguistics, and did my Ph.D. in French Philology, worked 7 years as a lecturer, assistant, researcher, and editor at the University of Zurich. I then moved to Italy and worked on several projects in Italy. I had obtained a 3-year research grant for advanced researchers and my husband and I moved to Italy, Florence. While I was doing research, my husband was taking care of our son who was born a year after our arrival in Italy.

When we moved to the Netherlands in 2005, my life shifted 180 degrees: I turned from sole breadwinner to accompanying partner (expat spouse) within 48 hours. – In the following years (!) I had a hard time accepting that I couldn't pursue my former career if I wanted to take care of my son. At that time we didn't have a network of trusted friends that would support us, so we could only rely on ourselves and an occasional babysitter to take care of by then three children. In the following years, I decided to learn new skills and assess those I already had, and I managed to find a new purpose: helping international families thrive during their life in another country. My volunteer work with expats helped me understand what they needed to lead a gratifying life. I became a Language Consultant and Intercultural Communication Trainer who helps internationals to understand their new culture and language while maintaining their home language.

I have experienced life in Switzerland, France, Italy, and the Netherlands, first as a child of expatriates, then as a student, as a researcher and sole breadwinner, and as an accompanying partner; as single, with a partner, with a child.

With every move and change of "home" was the opportunity to experience life in a new place, but one which came with the challenge of learning to assert myself in a new culture. People we meet in new cultural settings don't know who we are or what we are capable of, and it takes time to gain their trust and prove that we are trustworthy.

We can accelerate this process by being proactive, connecting with locals, building our new village that not only will be there for us if we need it but also for our children so that they can grow up in a community that will be their Ersatz-family. Learning the local language and the rules, values, and beliefs of the host culture need to come naturally. My mother used to tell us that as we are guests in the country, we need to adapt and integrate. It starts with learning the language, learning the rules of the society we live in, and by respecting the "otherness". If we can adopt what we like and what feels aligned with our convictions and beliefs, and understand and respect what is different, we can thrive in every place.

I managed to adapt and thrive in all the places I lived so far, by being proactive, learning the language, being curious and open-minded.

So far I have never lived in my parent's passport country and as a real expat (as of living out of the parent's passport country)-since-birth, I embrace this kind of life to the fullest and help others to do the same.

If you would like to have further information about how to lead a balanced and healthy life abroad, you can join the Families In Global Transition (FIGT) or follow me on my website www.utesinternationallounge.com

The 5 most common challenges a parent faces while raising a multicultural kid and how to address them

by Vivian Chiona, Dr. Brigitte Vittrup, Elisavet Arkolaki

A dialogue between a third culture child (TCK) and his classmate as published on expatnest.com. When the latter asked, "Where do you come from?", the TCK replied, "My father is from Brazil, my mother is from the States, my brother lives in Canada."

"And you are..?" the classmate asked.

"Blessed," he replied.

And blessed are our kids indeed! Recent studies now debunk old myths that predict isolation and confusion for children of mixed cultural heritage. On the contrary, they suggest that these children demonstrate a stronger appreciation for diversity. They develop an ability to understand multiple sides of controversial issues, thanks to their own multicultural heritage. They also appear to have enhanced creativity when it comes to problem-solving.

Before getting there though, as is the case for every child, the road that leads to a strong sense of self-identity can be bumpy. Identity is a complex thing, and for people of mixed cultural backgrounds, it can be even more difficult to define themselves and figure out where they belong. It can take a while before they are able to see themselves as whole persons, rather than a pie-chart, split up into percentages. It takes proper guidance and support from their family and community in order to grow up with pride, confidence and a strong sense of self.

When parents and professionals, who are here to give us pointers and assistance throughout our parenting journey, work together, we can expect our children to thrive.

1) Maintaining the minority language(s)

by Elisavet Arkolaki

One of the most common struggles comes in the form of maintaining the minority language(s) at the same level as the community language. There is still no world statistics but it is generally believed that more than half of the world's population is bilingual (source: https://www.ncbi.nlm.nih.gov/pmc/articles/PMC3322418/#R1). Even though multilingualism is as normal as monolingualism, yet, there is a genuine struggle to keep all spoken languages at the same level.

Traditionally, the "one person, one language" (OPOL) approach has been regarded as the best method for bilingual language acquisition. Though, as Chontelle Bonfiglio from 'Bilingual Kidspot' wrote, "Just because you speak to your child in your native language, it doesn't mean that they will automatically start to speak it back especially when everyone else around them is speaking another language. Sure they might understand everything you have said, but speaking back takes a lot more effort and sometimes children tend to go with the easier option." Each family is unique and we often need to follow different approaches in order to meet our family's needs.

An excellent resource is the article '40 tips for raising multilingual children' by Dr. Annabelle Humanes (Ph.D. in Bilingual Language Acquisition). Her children are exposed in four languages and she shares lots of research backed information on her website. Credible and well researched information can also be found on Dr. Ute Limacher-Riebold's website and Rita Rosenback's website.

2) Cultural Transition and Adaptation

by Vivian Chiona

Moving to a new culture can be a very stressful experience. The good news is that what appears challenging right now, will pay off in the long run. The majority of the kids who have been through such a transition eventually arrive at the conclusion that this experience helped them learn more about themselves and develop greater confidence in their ability to navigate new situations.

a) Healthy Goodbyes for Healthy Starts

According to Vivian Chiona, we often find ourselves avoiding proper closure or not knowing how to handle it. We need to accept and pass it on to our children, that going through the sadness of an ending is normal and healthy. "Goodbye" represents that closure and helps with a smoother transition. Closing the cycle gives you a strong foundation as you begin again. A healthy goodbye also helps you to savor the good parts of your experience; it holds these as treasures from your previous chapter and into your new one. This can give you strength; it can give you love. It can give you the power to continue when the transition is difficult.

A good idea is to turn the focus of the kids on the positive while anchoring and reassuring them about maintaining established relationships (ie communication via Skype until you meet again). In the meantime, help them recognize and accept all the emotions, good or bad, and process them. Give them space to express themselves. Vivian suggests that assertiveness is one of the greatest skills; being able to express what we think and feel without blaming others but focusing on ourselves, and with the good intention of making our relationships better and "more real".

b) Raising our children's cultural intelligence prior to the move

Cultural intelligence can be broadly broken into 3 sub-dimensions:

Cultural knowledge refers to our ability to understand what culture means and how it can affect our behavior;

Cultural skills describe the ability to learn from interactions with others, to expand our understanding of diversity and its consequences, and to modify our behavior to fit a specific situation;

Cultural metacognition is what helps us to better understand and be understood. It occurs when we reflect on the role that culture plays in explaining our own behavior and consciously think about using different ways of communicating when interacting with individuals from different cultural backgrounds.

Cultural intelligence is the competence that each and every one of us need to improve our interpersonal skills within a multicultural set-up.

The journey towards raising our children's cultural intelligence begins with the parents being positive and well prepared about the transition. It can be very helpful to talk to the children about the new culture and its communication style before expatriating thus minimizing the chances of a complete cultural shock. Much of the learning will happen when the family arrives at the new destination, but learning about it in advance helps the family members be more open-minded and less critical to the perceived differences.

When people from different countries interact, they project perceptions and feelings formed by their native culture. Without a basic knowledge of what culture is and how it affects our personality, people tend to get offended or feel like an outcast, or even unintentionally insult those who don't share their values.

Only when the perception filters are put aside, our understanding of other people and cultures broadens and expands. As a result, our relationships will deepen and our acceptance of diversity will bring us together. Acceptance towards ourselves and towards others is the key to happiness.

3) Where is Home?

by Elisavet Arkolaki

A well-known proverb says "Home is where the heart is" which can be interpreted as wherever our loved ones are, that is our home. Secondly, it can mean that a person's heart, their love, will always be tied to the place they live, the family home. For multicultural children, and in particular, the children that move from one place to another, the aim is to help them find a home within them, and carry it in their hearts wherever they go.

"The ache for home lives in all of us," writes Maya Angelou, "the safe place where we can go as we are and not be questioned." Marianna Pogosyan, in her article 'Finding Home Between Worlds', is well aware of the fact that for some, whose childhoods were scattered around the world, home is a tapestry of foreign memories. For some, whose answer to "Where are you from?" is all but straightforward, the home has more than one address. For some who call themselves Third Culture Kids (TCKs), the ache for home is constant and insatiable.

So how do we help our children who live in between worlds find out where home is for them?

As a starting point, I would recommend you watch an insightful TED talk titled 'Where is Home' by writer Pico Iyer, who himself has three or four "origins". He meditates on the meaning of home, the joy of traveling and the serenity of standing still. He contemplates the idea that home has more to do with a piece of your soul rather than soil.

Another inspirational TED talk that poses lots of questions, and challenges our perception of how and why things are in certain ways, is 'Don't ask where I'm from, ask where I'm a local' by writer Taiye Selasi.

Vivian Chiona, in her article 'How I Became My Home' talks about her own experience, how she found and redefined her very personal concept of 'home' and the process she went through.

Regardless of how you and your children will eventually define "home", what matters the most is to help the children find peace with where they are right now and where they are heading to in the future and to be able to enjoy their life without feeling like there is "always something missing".

It's important to introduce them early on to the concept that "Home" can be wherever they currently find themselves, but that it can also be who and how they are. Home is mostly a place within. Marianna Pogosyan on 'In Search of Home' (expatnest.com) reflects on what it takes to build a feeling of "home" in a new country and how we can begin to know that we've found it.

4) Dealing with Prejudice

by Dr. Brigitte Vittrup

Multicultural families are more likely to face prejudice from society, which entails preconceived, negatively-biased thoughts or beliefs. As a result, the most vulnerable members of the family unit, the children, can be severely affected. The family, the teachers, and the community need to stand up for them. We need to open a dialogue with the kids affected by prejudice but also with the kids who are prejudiced towards the ones that look or behave differently. But most important of all, we all need to be positive role models. Children absorb and understand much more about the world through our behavior rather than our words. When the two don't match, the children are left confused.

I wrote the article 'How silence can breed prejudice: A child development professor explains how and why to talk to kids about race'. There, I explain why it is of paramount importance to not shy away from but talk to our children about races, skin colors, differences, and diversity. I clarify that 'silence from the parents' side sends a very loud message to the children that this topic is taboo. While the intended message may be "Shhh... race is a sensitive topic in this country, so be careful what you say out loud because we don't want to offend anybody," what the child is more likely to hear is "Shhh... there's something wrong with these people, so let's not talk about them."

Silence about race-related topics is common among adults. Often this silence is inspired by discomfort (because race is often treated as a topic "we don't talk about"), lack of practice (many of today's adults did not grow up in homes where race-related issues were frequently discussed), and the desire for children to be color blind. Unfortunately, our society is not colorblind, and neither are the children. Research shows that children as young as age 3-4 have begun to develop ideas and attitudes about race and ethnicity, which later leads to biased perceptions. These biases are perpetuated by stereotyped portrayals of racial and ethnic minorities in the media. Therefore, if we as adults do not have intentional conversations with children about these issues, the children are left to figure it out on their own, and often that leads to inaccurate and often biased ideas. In addition, silence about race-related issues can send the unintended message that the status quo (prejudice, inequality, and discrimination) is normal and okay. In addition, children whose parents do not discuss these topics are more likely to perceive their parents as being biased, and this, in turn, can influence their own development of racial biases.

In my research, I have asked many parents and teachers about the types of race-related conversations they have with children. Often, the responses include statements such as "It doesn't matter what people look like," "We're all the same on the inside," and "God loves everyone." These are well-intended statements, but unfortunately, they don't convey any practical messages to children about race or culture. To be effective, conversations have to be direct, explicit, and continuous across time.

When talking to children about race-related issues:

- Be honest and factual. You may not always have the answer to children's questions, but that is okay. If you have to look up information or even say "I don't know – let's find out", it leads children to believe that their questions are valid, and this is a topic that is okay to discuss.
- Present the information in an age-appropriate manner. Young children understand the concepts of fairness and being nice to others. Older children understand more complex concepts about stereotypes, prejudice, and discrimination.
- Ask children what they know and what they think. State the facts and engage children in conversation. For example, "Some people don't like….", "Some people think that [minority group] are…", "Have you seen/heard [news, events, experiences]?" and then ask "What do you think about that?" or "What would you say/do if you saw/heard…?"
- Use books, videos, websites, or news stories as springboards for conversations. Discuss the topics presented and then branch off to discuss how this relates to your own life and experiences, about what is right and wrong, and what we can do to make things better.

We need to deal with our own personal discomfort and engage our children in a conversation on these issues. Subjects that we might consider as 'sensitive' are in fact the most important ones to be addressed. The objective here is not to come up with the perfect answers; there aren't any.

Note from the editor: it's also worth reading Erin Winkler's article 'Here's How To Raise Race-Conscious Children'.

5) When a child expresses negative emotions

by Vivian Chiona

It is important to pass on the message of embracing and celebrating the blessings of expat life. It is also essential to convey an optimistic message: that these uncomfortable feelings will lessen over time. This too shall pass... Every thought, form, feeling, and situation in life is temporary. Isn't it comforting to know that one's sadness will have an end?

Here's a story to tell your child that contains this pearl of wisdom:

According to an old Sufi fable, there was once a king in the Middle East who was constantly torn between happiness and despair. The slightest thing would provoke a strong reaction in him. When he felt happy, it would swiftly turn into disappointment or hopelessness.

The king eventually became so tired of this that he decided to call for help. He was notified of a man in his kingdom who was said to be enlightened. The king pleaded for the wise man's help. When the wise man arrived to see the king, the latter said: "I want to be as you are. I want balance and clarity in my life – and I will pay you any price you demand for that insight."

The wise man responded: "I might be able to help you, but this insight is so valuable that the entirety of your kingdom would not be enough to pay for it. That's why I will give it to you as a gift if you will honor it."

The king agreed, and the wise man went on his way.

Weeks later, the wise man returned to the king, bringing with him a golden ring with these words inscribed on it: "This too shall pass."

"What is the meaning of this?" the king asked, baffled. The wise man told him to always carry this ring on him and to look at it before he judged any situation again. "Do this and peace will be with you always," the wise man said.

So, this too shall pass... Every thought, form, feeling, and situation in life is temporary. Isn't it comforting to know that your sadness will have an end? Yes, this too shall pass, just as other sad moments in the past have done. And isn't it a treasure to learn to appreciate every single moment of happiness is precious? This awareness of knowing that all things have an end – that no matter the situation, it will pass – gives us both the strength to carry on and the wisdom to enjoy what we have.

5 mistakes parents make when trying to raise bilingual children

by Rita Rosenback

When I was born, way back then in a little village in Finland, my circumstances made me predestined to grow up bilingual. Why do I say this? My parents, unbeknown to them, used a very effective way of passing on their respective mother tongues. My mother was from a 100% Finnish-speaking family and only ever spoke Finnish with me. My father, while fluent in Finnish, preferred Swedish. To be exact, he – like every Swedish-speaker around me – spoke a Finland-Swedish dialect, which is very different from standard Swedish. The majority language of our village was the Swedish dialect, so this is what I used with all my paternal relatives and neighbors. My parents spoke Finnish between them, so this gave me a little more exposure to Finnish, as did the frequent visits to my maternal relatives in the neighboring village. Not until I started school at the age of seven, did I learn to speak standard Swedish.

So ingrained in me was the routine of speaking Swedish with my father and Finnish with my mother that when writing a postcard to them during my first solo trip abroad, I did it in both languages with every second word in Finnish and Swedish. I felt that either my mother or father would feel that the card was for the other parent should I have written the card only in one language. I was 19 at the time, and my bilingual upbringing had left a strong mark on my language preferences.

My parents did what came naturally to them when they chose the languages they spoke with me and my brother. They did this without reading any books or anybody advising them, and it worked out beautifully. Both my brother and I became fluent bilinguals in Swedish and Finnish. Shouldn't the same apply to any other family where more than one language is spoken? Unfortunately not. For example, had my mother been bilingual, she might well have chosen to speak Swedish too, to make life easier. In that case, my brother and I would probably have struggled with learning Finnish at school, like most of our peers did.

There are many ways to raise children to speak the family languages, but there are some aspects that are crucial to a successful multilingual upbringing. Having connected with thousands of parents in multilingual families, here are some of the most common mistakes I have come across that parents might make when passing on more than one language to their kids.

a) Believing that their child will automatically become bilingual

Just like me, many bilinguals have grown up to naturally master the family languages, without anyone paying too much attention to the process: the circumstances happened to be ideal. This can however not be taken for granted. Just because a family uses two (or more) languages does not mean that the children will automatically learn to speak them. The children may become what is known as passive or receptive bilinguals which means that they understand the family languages but only speak the community language.

- It doesn't happen by magic!

b) Not being consistent

To be in with the best possible chance of successfully raising their child to become bilingual, parents should try to be consistent in their language use. Research has shown that children whose parents readily switch from one language to another are more likely to stop using the minority language with their parents. This usually happens at the point when the children get more exposure to the community language through nursery or school. If parents have maintained a consistent language pattern at home the chances are considerably higher that the minority language will continue to be a language in active use for the children. The importance of consistency grows the less exposure there is to a language. In a family with an equal amount of exposure to both/all languages, there is less need for consistency in language choice.

- Language: choose it and use it and you won't lose it!

c) Giving up too easily

There are several obstacles to overcome when bringing up a bilingual child. Parents need to be committed to the task, so these challenges don't derail them. The best thing to do is to learn about the possible hurdles in advance and be aware of the myths surrounding bilingual children – and most of all, having the confidence to continue when it feels like there is no progress.

- Don't be the parent who failed to plan!

d) Leaving it until later

While it is never too late to learn a language (as a child or even as an adult), it is true that the earlier a child starts to learn the family languages the easier the journey is. Waiting until the child has learned the community language means that the family is used to only speaking the community language, a pattern that is not easy to change.

- Leave it until later and later may never come!

e) Not seeking help and support

Being a parent is not a walk in the park at the best of times. Throwing an extra language or two into the mix does not make it any easier. It is sad to see children miss out on growing up learning more than one language and being able to speak with their grandparents or other relatives. The situation could have been different, had the parents sought advice on how to make sure that the family languages are passed on to the next generation.

- A wise parent asks for advice when needed!

Language delays in multilingual children: what are they and what to do about them

by Dr. Mary-Pat O'Malley-Keighran

The first important thing to know is that speaking two or more languages does not cause any speech and language delays or disorders. If your child has a problem with speech or language, it's not because they're multilingual. Being multilingual doesn't make speech and language problems worse. Children who have autism or Down syndrome can and do become multilingual. If your family needs two or more languages to communicate and connect, then that's what they need. Never follow the advice to drop a language in the belief that it will simplify things. It won't. It might even make things worse as you cut off one set of language skills. Like trying to only use your right hand and not your left. Your multilingual child's language development is distributed across the languages. Meaning that sometimes, they will know words in one language but not the other. Balance is an illusion because language doesn't work that way.

Here are five amazing facts about your bilingual baby's brain and language development:

#1 Your baby starts to hear at around 26 weeks of your pregnancy. Now, of course, this isn't exactly like hearing on the outside! Sound has to pass through skin and muscle and amniotic fluid. But research shows that babies can tell the difference between sounds like /b/ and /z/ before they are even born. Distinguishing one language from another in a bilingual baby is robust at birth. They show language preferences at birth and shortly after for languages they heard while still on the inside! Your bilingual baby's language journey starts before they're born!

#2 Newborn babies show a preference for stories that were read to them before they were born. They also show a preference for their mother's voice at birth. Only a few days after birth, newborn babies respond differently to language and to non-language sounds. Very young infants prefer to listen to speech over non-speech sounds.

#3 Babies are born with the ability to distinguish between and produce all of the sounds in all of the world's languages! That's around 600 consonants and 200 vowels! Starting at about 6 months of age, this ability gradually starts to narrow to the languages in their environment.

#4 Babies learn language rules earlier than you think! All languages have rules for what sounds can go together to make syllables and words. Like in English, we don't have words that start with /nd/. But Swahili has words that begin with this combination of consonants. At 9 months of age, babies have been found to show a preference for what is called legal combinations of sounds in their languages.

#5 Babies don't just learn languages by listening. Looking at your face is important too. There's research to show that 6 and 8-month-old bilingual babies could distinguish between French and English speakers just by looking at speakers on videos with the sound turned down.

And here are three important things to remember about how language works in multilingual children. Keeping these in mind will save you a lot of heartache! (Thanks to Kathryn Kohnert for pointing them out in her 2010 paper listed in the resources at the end of the chapter).

#1 Language skills tend to be distributed across languages and vary over time. This means that it's natural for multilingual children to know a word in only one of their languages. It's not a case of two or three monolingual speakers of each language in the one child. A simple example is where they have words to do with home and family and community in the language used there and then they learn words to do with maths and science and geography and so on at school. It's important to know this because it means you need to think about all of the words your child has in all of their languages. And it means that if they're seeing a speech and language therapist, they need to have all of their languages tested. When their language is tested, it's not unusual for multilingual children to do better on some things than on others. So, they might be good with vocabulary and story-telling in the home language and not so good at these in the community language, especially when they've just started school.

2 The languages interact with each other. Basically, the languages do seem to be stored separately in multilingual children's brains, but they interact with each other. Multilingual people tend to mix languages and switch between them to different degrees. Children aren't confused when they mix. You can only mix things that are separate, to begin with, and if you look closely, the mixed things they say are grammatically correct. It might be that they didn't have the word they wanted in one language, so they pop in the equivalent word from another language - pretty cool when you think about it.

#3 Everyone's different and every multilingual situation is unique. In the research, even when children are matched closely in groups, there's a lot of variation between individual children in the group and how they perform on language testing.

And there's also a lot of variation between groups of carefully matched multilingual children who speak the same languages. That's because there is a range of factors that affect language development which is unique for every family. Things like the number of languages spoken, the ages at which children are exposed to the different languages, the opportunities they have to use the languages, their own motivation which can change over time, how similar or different the languages are, the social value attached to the languages and so on. Assessment of multilingual children's speech & language skills need to take these three factors into account. Here's an example of the kind of variation I mean: a boy's expressive vocabulary can vary from 79 words to 511 words at 24 months of age and still be considered within normal limits!

You need to know the difference between speech and language too. Speech means the actual sounds your child is using like /p/ or /s/, how they are pronouncing words (saying tar when they mean car or boon when they mean spoon), having an accent, how their voice sounds, are they stuttering and so on.

Language is about understanding what you're saying to them, following instructions, their vocabulary, how many words they're using, the different kinds of words they're using (nouns, verbs, adjectives, prepositions) combining words together to make phrases and sentences, telling stories, jokes, switching between languages and so on. You need to know about language comprehension and expression or expressive language. Comprehension is what a child understands. You say 'Get your coat and hat and scarf' (without pointing to them or without having said 'We're going for a walk') and they go get them for example. Expression is what they say- the words they use- not how they pronounce them but words and phrases like: mama gone, look mama, birdie, I do it, and so on.

In this chapter, I'm going to focus on language problems in multilingual children. If you'd like to read more about speech problems in multilingual children, be sure to visit my blog at www.talknua.com

So, when it comes to your child's language development, you might be worried that your child is slow to start talking or that she doesn't seem to use a lot of words. You might have come across expressions like late talkers, late language learners or language delay or late language emergence. I'm going to use the term late talkers as that's what the American Speech, Language, & Hearing Association are currently using. Let's take a look at what the current research has to say.

What exactly is late talking?

Leslie Rescorla, a researcher in this area, says expressive language delay is like fever: it's a symptom found in many conditions like children with hearing loss or cleft palate. That makes diagnosing children who are late to talk challenging. But here we're talking about late talkers who don't have other conditions like autism or Down syndrome. Children who are late talkers can be late in expression only, or they can have a delay that is a mixture of a delay in comprehension and expression.

Basically, children are considered late talkers when they are between 18 and 35 months old, understanding what you say to them but they're using a limited number of words (It's called having limited expressive vocabulary). This means that they don't use a lot of words or a lot of different kinds of words (nouns, verbs, prepositions) and word combinations. To be considered a late talker, all other areas of development need to be typical - things like their play and when they walked, hearing, and so on. However, life isn't always as straightforward as the research and some late talkers might have a delay in understanding as well. Overall, the outlook is good for late talkers with most of them moving into the average range on language tests by preschool. Early identification is important. A slow start to vocabulary is more likely to be short-lived if it's identified before 18 months and is the only issue your child has. At 24 months, 50-70% of children could catch up to their peers. But, one study showed that 82% of toddlers who failed language screenings at 30 months were not recovering by age 6. In general, children who were late talkers do continue to do more poorly on language testing in school. This means they're at risk for language disorders. (These are called Specific Language Impairment (SLI) or Developmental Language Disorders (DLD). These problems are persistent language problems that tend to be diagnosed after age 4).

What might this look like in your child though? Well, if your child is 24 months old and does not yet use 50 words or two-word combinations, they'd be considered late talkers. Elizabeth Peña, another established researcher, says that between 18-20 months, you should expect your child to be using AT LEAST 10 words and those words would be distributed across the languages. So they might have more words in one language than the other. It's the total amount you're interested in.

First words usually come any time from 8 – 15 months depending on what you read. At first, growth is slow with 18-month-old children learning about 10 new words per month. (Don't get too hung up on the numbers though. There's so much variation between children when it comes to early language development that there are only rough guides. And it's also important to think about what they're using the words for. It's all about communication - so are they requesting something like tickling to be repeated or stopped, are they protesting, rejecting something, commenting, and so on). Between 17 & 20 months, there's a rapid vocabulary spurt as they approach the 50-word mark and they learn several new words daily. Not all children go through this vocabulary spurt though. Most of the ages and stages that you come across are based on monolingual children but the milestones are similar for bilingual children. Children make progress at different rates but it is important to see steady progress.

How common is late talking?

Again, estimates vary but ASHA reports that between 10-20% of children at the age of 2 present with slow onset and development of their expressive language. In 18- to 23-month-old toddlers, the percentage of late talkers is estimated to be 13.5%. This rate rises to 16%-17.5% in 30- to 36-month-old children. If we're talking about children who have problems with understanding and using language, then the rate is about 13.4%. If children have a family who have had a speech or language problem, then the rate is 23% compared to those with no family history (12%). Boys are three times more likely than girls to have late language emergence.

The estimated proportion of late talkers who go on to develop persistent language problems varies widely from 6%- 44% depending on the study. It's also important to remember that late talking is a characteristic or feature of a child's development. It's not a disorder or a diagnostic or a label. It's a description. And remember too that the most likely outcome for individual children who are late to talk is that they will catch up to their typically developing peers.

Do they grow out of it?

Another hard question to answer but about 50% of late talkers do score in the normal range by age 3 on vocabulary measures and in the normal range of grammar and conversational skills by school age. Late bloomers is the name given to children who catch up in the 3-5-year-old period. (Approximately 50% to 70% of late talkers are reported to catch up to peers and demonstrate normal language development by late preschool and school-age.) There's some research suggesting that late bloomers use more communicative gestures than age-matched late talkers who remained delayed. Using communicative gestures allows them to compensate for limited oral expressive vocabulary. Research also indicates that late bloomers are less likely to have language comprehension delays (in addition to the expressive language delay) when compared with children who remain delayed. In one study, the presence of language impairment at age 7 was 20% for children with a history of late language emergence compared with 11% for controls. That is, only one in five late talkers had language impairment at age 7. One of the best resources I've come across for gestures is First Words Project. You can find a list of 16 gestures that your child should be using by 16 months. You'll need to think about which ones are part of your culture and which ones aren't.

BUT and it's a big one, there's research showing that children who had expressive language delay between 24 and 31 months of age had weaker language skills throughout their adolescence. Even though they had language scores in the average range, they were still performing more poorly than their peers on vocabulary, grammar, and verbal memory. And there's also research showing that where children have delays in understanding and expression together, they can struggle with learning to read. How much a toddler understands may be a better predictor of expressive language outcome than how much she or he says. Late talkers are at relatively low risk for language or learning disorders. And the majority of children with SLI/DLD are not former late talkers. Being a late talker is a risk factor for language or learning disorders but it is neither a clinical condition nor a certain sign of disorder to come. One author, Rhea Paul recommends that late talkers who also have trouble with language comprehension or understanding should receive intervention while children who don't struggle with comprehension should receive only occasional monitoring of language growth.

It's still difficult though to predict accurately which late talkers are likely to have long-term problems. Children who aren't combining words at 24 months appear to have worse outcomes than children who don't produce any words at 15 months (this is not a perfect predictor though -so frustrating- I know!).

Outcomes tend to be poorer for children who have problems with comprehension as well as expression, who don't communicate using gestures and who don't imitate body movements. Laura Mize is an American pediatric speech and language therapist with loads of great free resources on her website www.teachmetotalk.com

Prediction gets more accurate as children get older: in 4-year-olds, the greater the number of areas of language that are affected, the more likely it is that the problems will persist into school age. Areas of language means comprehension, grammar (like sentence structure, word structure), story-telling. If your child still has language problems at age 5 and over, these problems do tend to persist. Children who start school with oral language problems are at risk of reading problems and poor academic attainments. The gaps in their language tend not to close over time. Again if comprehension and non-verbal ability are affected, the language outcomes tend to be poor.

And you can't know in advance if your child's going to be a late bloomer. It's definitely not a good idea to take a chance on the possibility of them growing out of it. It's hard to predict who will grow out of it and who won't. The children who are at greatest risk for not growing out of it are those where there's a family history of language delay, where their comprehension is also delayed, and where they use few gestures. The best gestures for language development are ones that add meaning. What does that mean? It's shaking their head while saying 'water'. In effect, they're saying 'no water' or 'I don't want water'. The gesture expands the meaning of the word. Shaking your head while saying 'no' doesn't expand the meaning of the word.

One research paper that looked at 20 studies involving 2134 children, found that the significant predictors of expressive language outcomes included expressive vocabulary size at toddlerhood (up to age 36 months), language comprehension, and socioeconomic status (usually measured by looking at parents' levels of education and mothers' level of education in particular. Predictors that were not significant were the child's gender, using phrases, and having a family history of speech & language problems.

Why do some children start to talk later than others?

No clear answer to this question yet. Early language development varies from one child to another. But, things that late talkers tend to have in common are things like a family history of early language delay, being a boy, being born at less than 85% of their optimal birth weight or at less than 37 weeks of pregnancy.

What if we have home languages that are different from the language used in my child's school?

In this situation, let's say you speak Polish at home and your child starts preschool with very little English. Or you arrive in an English-speaking country and your child starts school with very little English. It's important to remember that language learning takes time. A long time! And you need to think about what aspects of language you mean. So being able to have a conversation with a friend while you play a game is different from the language you need in order to be able to do maths problems for example. If you're learning the school language as a second or additional language, you're not at the same starting point as children who have learned only that language since birth. And it's not helpful to compare your child to monolingual children. That's like comparing apples and oranges & it's not accurate. If your child hasn't had enough exposure to the school language, they may need support with it but not because they have a language disorder.

When should I see a speech & language therapist (SLP)?

The Hanen Centre, which is based in Canada, suggests that your child needs to see an SLT if

- they're 18 months old and not using at least 20 words, including different types of words, such as nouns or names of things (cup, biccie for biscuit), verbs or doing words (eat, go), prepositions or location words (up, down), adjectives or describing words (hot, mine), and social words (hi, bye). They need different types of words so that they can combine them into phrases like want biccie.

Or

- they're 24-month-olds and they aren't using at least 100 words and combining 2 words together. The word combinations need to be original. Phrases like Thank you. I want to, all gone, what's that? are not genuine phrases. They're chunks that are learned as one unit. Examples of real word combinations come from the child themselves, that they haven't heard before. Things like: "kitty gone", or "dirty dress".

The research suggests that we can reliably identify language delay at 24 months. But you need to take into consideration how long waiting lists in your country are. It's never too early to have the referral made to an SLT. We can assess children from a very young age. And it's better to be referred and not need the referral than need it and be stuck on a waiting list. Please listen to your instinct and ignore comments like 'Oh he's too young to see an SLT'. That's just not true! A recent multinational study involving 59 professionals from psychology, education, SLT, pediatrics and child psychiatry says that healthcare professionals should rely on concerns expressed by the people who know the child well. And the outcomes for children where the diagnosis is made later are not as positive as when the problem is identified early. The research shows that younger children make greater progress in their language development with intervention. But, language disorders that are evident at age 5 tend to stay fairly stable throughout the school years.

Find out more about what we do here www.talknua.com/about/. Ideally, you want an SLT who has experience working with bilingual families. If that's not possible, read this post http://talknua.com/the-3-times-you-should-definitely-ignore-your-doctor/ before you go so you'll be prepared.

Is it because we speak more than one language?

Definitely not! More people in the world speak two languages or more but most of the research tends to involve children who speak one language. Your child's language development is affected by the amount and quality of input they get and the opportunities they have to use the language(s) they have. But speaking more than one language does not cause even a temporary delay in language development. What's important is to describe what languages your child is exposed to, who they speak them with, and a rough idea of how much exposure to and use of each language is typical for your child. Please don't compare the development of your child's languages to that of other children. Each family is unique and comparisons are not helpful unless the language environment and experience are the same - and that's unique to each child. And don't compare them to monolingual children either. It's not a legitimate comparison. Elizabeth Peña says bilingualism is like cake. If you make raspberry-apple cake for example, both flavors are unique and together they enhance the flavor of the whole. The cake isn't one or the other. It's a unique combination.

What can you do to help? Here are 7 ideas to get you started:

#1 Get a referral to an SLT and preferably one who is experienced in working with multilingual families. Don't accept advice to drop a home language. This suggestion is not supported by any research and is not best practice. Don't feel under pressure to follow a one person one language (OPOL) approach either, as this isn't the only or the most effective way to nurture multilingual development and it can feel somewhat unnatural. In terms of intervention for young children, it's generally done through the parents, showing you how to best encourage your child's language development. And these parent-implemented interventions work. It's worth getting in early as the benefits go beyond vocabulary to grammar, reading & writing, academic performance, and communication.

#2 Get your child's hearing checked just to make sure it's as it should be.

#3 If you're worried that your child's expressive language is not progressing, set aside 30 minutes a day where your sole focus is on interacting with them. In this 30 minute period, you want to observe them closely and see what they are interested in. What are they looking at? Playing with? Children's language develops better when we give them the name for the thing they're looking at or the action they're doing than when we try to direct their attention to what we're interested in. So it should sound something like: Oh, you're walking to the sofa. Plop! You sat down! And not like this: Look, Jamie, here's a book. Look at the book. This small action consistently taken will make a difference.

4 Keep a communication diary. Now don't panic. It doesn't have to be anything fancy, just somewhere you can write down how they communicate. So it can be that they use their whole body, they move away to say I don't want that. Or they use a word with a gesture like shaking their head and saying "No". You also want to look at what they're communicating about. These are called communicative intentions and are really important because vocabulary is not enough. They need experience using the words they've got to communicate about what's important to them. So, this includes things like: greeting you when you come home, indicating farewell or goodbye, requesting action like holding his hands up to communicate Pick me up, rejecting something, commenting. These can be done using words or gestures or whole-body movements. You want to see new words appearing over the course of a month.

5 Record the different types of words your child uses. So, what nouns, verbs, adjectives, prepositions and so on. Diversity in your child's vocabulary in terms of the different types of words is important. They need nouns and verbs in order to put two words together. Keep a record of the different types of words that your child is using in all of their languages - the names of things like animals, family members, pets, toys, favorite characters, etc. For tips on how to build your child's noun vocabulary, read this

http://talknua.com/why-is-your-childs-vocabulary-development-important/. (It's totally normal for children to have a word in one language and not in another).

There is research showing that children who use a range of different verbs develop better when it comes to grammar than children who use a more restricted range of verbs. You need to think about the verbs in all of your child's languages. For more details about verbs and how to develop your child's verb vocabulary, read this http://talknua.com/the-neglected-words-in-your-childs-early-vocabulary/.

6 Gestures are really important for language development. Check out the excellent First Words Project website and especially the 16X16 series here www.firstwordsproject.com

#7 Look at books together. Look is the important word here. You don't have to read the book to encourage an interest in books and boost language development. The idea is that you use the book as a conversation starter with your child. You can find 18 ways to make the most of books with your child here http://talknua.com/19-ways-to-read-books/ and 40 book ideas for reading together here http://talknua.com/40-fabulous-reads-for-you-your-children/.

If you'd like more tips about speech, language, and communication, be sure and sign up at www.talknua.com

References

- Bishop, DVM, Snowling, M., Thompson, P., Greenhalgh, T, & the CATALISE consortium. (2016) CATALISE: a multinational and multidisciplinary Delphi consensus study: identifying language impairments in children. PLOS One 11(7): e0158753.doi:10.137/journal.pone.0158753

- Bishop, DVM, Snowling, M., Thompson, P., Greenhalgh, T, & the CATALISE consortium. (2016) Phase 2 of CATALISE: a multinational and multidisciplinary Delphi consensus study of problems with language development: terminology. Journal of Child Psychology & Psychiatry 58(10): 1068-1080.
- Byers-Heinlen, K., Burns, T., & Werker, J. (2010). Monolingual, bilingual, trilingual: infants' language experience influences the development of a word learning heuristic. Developmental Science 12(5): 815-823.
- Byers-Heinlen, K., Burns, T., & Werker, J. (2010). The roots to bilingualism in newborns. Psychological Science 2 (3): 343-348.
- Byers-Heinlen, K., Morin-Lessard, E., & Lew-Williams, C. (2017). Bilingual infants control their languages as they listen. Proceedings of the National Academy of Sciences of the United States of America, 114(34): 9032-9037.
- Capone-Singleton, N. (2018). Late Talkers: Why the Wait-and-See approach is outdated. Paediatric Clinics of North America 65: 13-29.
- Everitt, A., Hannaford, P., and Conti-Ramsden, T. (2013). Markers for persistent specific expressive language delay in 3-4 year olds. International Journal of Language and Communication Disorders 48(3): 534-553.
- Fisher, E. (2017). A systematic review and meta-analysis of predictors of expressive-language outcomes among late talkers. Journal of Speech, Language, and Hearing Research 60: 2935-2948.
- Hadley, P, Rispoli, M. &, Hsu, N. (2016) Toddlers' verb lexicon diversity and grammatical outcomes. Language, Speech, and Hearing Services in Schools 47: 44-58.
- Hawa, V. and Spanoudis, G. (2014) Toddlers with delayed expressive language: an overview of the characteristics, risk factors, and language outcomes. Research Developmental Disabilities 35: 400-407.
- Kohnert, K. (2010). Bilingual children with primary language impairment: Issues, evidence and implications for clinical actions. Journal of Communication Disorders 43: 456-473.

- Late Language Emergence Overview
  https://www.asha.org/Practice-Portal/Clinical-Topics/Late-Language-Emergence/

- Rescorla, L. (2013). Late talkers: do good predictors of outcome exist? Developmental Disabilities Research Reviews 17:141-150.

- The Hanen Centre
  http://www.hanen.org/helpful-info/articles/how-to-tell-if-your-child-is-a-late-talker-%E2%80%93-and-w.aspx

- Rice, M. Taylor, C. & Zubric, S. (2008) Language outcomes of 7 year old children with or without a history of late language emergence at 24 months. Journal of Speech, Language, and Hearing Research 50(2): 394-407.

- Werker, J., & Byers-Heinlen, K., & Fennell, C. (2009). Bilingual beginnings to learning words. Philosophical Transactions of the Royal Society. 364: 3649-3663.

- Zambrana, I., Pons, F., Eadie, P., and Ystrom, E. (2014). Trajectories of language delay from age 3-5: persistence, recovery, and late onset. International Journal of Language & Communication Disorders 49(3): 304-316.

Raising multilingual children with additional needs abroad

by Dr. Ute Limacher-Riebold

One of the longest-lasting myths concerning multilingualism is that children with additional needs should not become multilingual, or if they already are using a minority language at home, they should stop using it. Thanks to new research in the field, this view is to be replaced by one that states that these children can indeed become multilingual, or remain so.

Multilingual Children with additional needs living abroad

Transmitting a heritage language while living abroad requires dedication, consistency and time. The challenge for parents is even greater if the children need additional support. It is arduous for parents to find suitable support, even when they are familiar with the system. The whole process is even more tedious for those who have to navigate an unfamiliar system and have to find out about the regulations, policies and practices in another language. Many parents feel vulnerable and disoriented.

Millie's story

Millie Slavidou, a British mother of three, currently living in Cyprus, shared her experience in an interview on my site.

Millie is a linguist and knows about language acquisition and learning, as well as about multilingualism. She is aware of the possibilities, the best practices and strategies, and of what is realistic and what not, and she knows what and where to search for answers and advice. Her personal experience illustrates what experts in the field can go through when navigating the system with a child that needs additional support.

Millie's family speaks multiple languages. Millie and her husband raise their children abroad and want them to become fluent in all their languages.

Millie has now been living in Cyprus for three years (2019) and prior to this spent some years in Italy and lived in Greece for 16 years. She speaks English, Greek and Italian fluently, and studied linguistics in Britain. With her three children, she speaks exclusively English at home and sometimes throws in a phrase in Italian. Her youngest son "has additional needs that are severe enough that he has been going to speech therapy for many years. He also has cognitive delays." She shares the beginning of her journey by describing how arduous her experience was with getting a referral for a speech therapist in Greece. She was told that he "can't have speech therapy because you are bilingual and this is what is causing the problem". Millie was warned, that by insisting on wanting to raise her son bilingually, she was sabotaging him, and even though her "other two children were doing well and had very good age-appropriate vocabulary in both their languages", she was told that "children with additional needs cannot be bilingual", therefore she was supposedly causing the problem for her third child. It was only thanks to her determination that she managed, against all odds, to obtain speech therapy for her son.

Parents sometimes have to fight to get the therapy their children need. Many parents believe healthcare professionals, teachers etc because they are supposed to know how to best support AN children, and don't question their advice. They accept that in order to support their children with the community language, they should stop speaking their own language with their children.

Millies' son received the speech therapy he needed in the end, but some of the health practitioners still insisted that she should "stop bilingualism" and speak the community language with him instead. It took her many attempts to find professionals that would accept her talking her language with him. When her son started school, Millie got told again by the teacher to "stop speaking English" with her son.

What should be the most obvious and natural thing to do – speaking your language with your child – becomes the scapegoat whenever a multilingual child has any kind of AN issue. The number of languages is the first thing people blame and consider responsible. When children of multilingual families struggle with acquiring language and/or with becoming verbal, the "too many" languages are blamed.

Millie's son never attended nursery school because he was refused due to his issues. It is only thanks to Millie's tireless perseverance that he got into school: "You have to be quite strong to deal with this. Some people can't. I resent being patronized by doctors because they assume that you don't know anything. They speak to you as if you were completely ignorant and I know what can be done, I know what I'm talking about. You really feel you're fighting an uphill battle."

Millie and her family are now well settled in Cyprus, where the system for children with additional needs at primary school is supportive. Her son is nine years old and goes to a special unit within the mainstream school and receives the support he needs. Teachers and speech therapists managed to collaborate, and together with Millies' support, her son is making great progress.

When families lack support in this kind of situation while living abroad, they do not always have the resources and means to move internationally. Millie says that one of the reasons why they moved to Cyprus was that they speak Greek there too and that her husband was very concerned about putting their son into a new linguistic environment. They were worried about the impact of an additional – fourth – language on their son's overall development. In Cyprus, the underlying culture is Greek, which her son is very familiar with, and which certainly contributed to his smooth adaptation to the new setting. – For children with AN, change can be very difficult and parents need to take this into consideration when they face changes such as an international move.

Millie's 4 tips for families in a similar situation:

1) **Trust your own instincts:** You're not harming your child when you speak your own language with him.

2) **Be prepared:** You have to do the research about the bilingualism aspect, you have to research your child's condition, whatever the condition is, because you might come up against a brick wall, with people being negative about it and you need to be informed. – Don't expect speech therapists, teachers and doctors to know the solution suitable for your child. They are simply human beings. There is a lot of new research data about bilingualism, multilingualism and the function of the brain. But not everyone is aware of all these research results.

3) **You have to stand up:** Over and over again, you have to stand up for your child. It can be difficult but you should ignore the inner voice that holds you back: go for it and keep going. – There are other children born with the same or similar

condition as your child, and their parents will also need some support and they'll need help, maybe you can be part of that help in some way.

4) Join online communities for parents of children with all kinds of conditions:

Children with additional needs are very common, and one doesn't need to hide it. There is nothing to be ashamed of. Some of these online groups are very knowledgeable, they might refer you to a paper, a piece of research, you can really find a lot of help from them! – It is important to join these groups not only to gather information but also because you will need to feel that you're not the only one who is dealing with this.

Tips for parents with multilingual AN children living abroad

The general fear of professionals and parents alike, when it comes to multilingualism and children with additional needs, is that learning one language is already difficult for these children, therefore learning two or more languages would be just too difficult. They wonder if exposing a child with AN to two or more languages would result in no language being learned well:

"This is a myth and it has been debunked through studies of typically developing children and children from the three groups [specific (or primary) language impairment (SLI), Down Syndrome (DS) and Autism Spectrum Disorder (ASD)]. Children with developmental disabilities, regardless of diagnosis, can and do become bilingual, but, unfortunately, many professionals and families are not aware of these research findings."

Many studies disprove the notion that children with developmental disabilities or speech impairments should stop using their heritage language and focus only on one language. Bilingualism does not increase the risk or severity of language impairment (Peña 2016, 87), and impairment status is not related to bilingualism, because risk factors for impairment and their level of severity are similar for both monolingual and dual language learners (DLL) children.

Fortunately, the number of professionals knowing that children with language or cognitive impairment are capable of learning two (or more) languages is increasing.

In 2005, Tamar Kremer-Sadlik from the University of California, Los Angeles, pointed out that there is no proof that multilingualism harms language acquisition or further language learning in impaired or delayed children.

In a special issue of the Journal of Communication Disorders (2016), researchers presented their results about bilingual access and participation for children with developmental disabilities. They focused on three groups: children with specific (or primary) language impairment (SLI), Down Syndrome (DS) and Autism Spectrum Disorder (ASD), as "these are the ones who have been studied to any real degree with the emphasis having been put on bilingual children with SLI. Almost no research exists on bilingualism in other populations of children with developmental disabilities such as children with cerebral palsy or intellectual disabilities or other etiologies." (Elizabeth Kay-Raining Bird, Psychology Today)

The study by Korkoman M. et al (2012) on simultaneous bilingualism and its possible impact on language problems finds that:

"Simultaneous bilingualism does not aggravate specific language problems but may result in slower development of vocabulary both in children with and without specific language problems. Considering also advantages, a bilingual upbringing is an option also for children with specific language problems. In assessment, tests of vocabulary may be sensitive to bilingualism, instead tests assessing comprehension, syntax and nonword repetition may provide less biased methods." (Korkoman et al 2012)

Fact is: Children with AN can learn multiple languages (simultaneously and sequentially)

Multilingual children will acquire at least one additional language during their first years of life without formal education (simultaneous multilinguals) or learn the additional language(s) in formal education (sequential multilinguals), or there can be a combination of both: i.e. acquire two languages at a very early stage and learn additional languages later. They can speak and/or read and write all their languages to a certain degree of fluency at some point of their life, and one or more of their languages can become dominant, whereas others, that might have been dominant before, become less dominant or even passive (this is called language shift and language attrition).

Is there a difference between simultaneous and sequential bilinguals with AN?

Compared with monolingual peers, **simultaneous bilinguals** with developmental disabilities show no difference in language skills when compared in an appropriate way. This means that for simultaneous bilinguals with a developmental disability who have relatively equal abilities in both languages, research shows that their ability in each language does not differ from that of monolingual similarly affected peers.

However, many simultaneous bilingual children do not have equal abilities in both or all their languages because they hear and use one language more often than the other. When this happens, the stronger language should be taken as a reference. Ideally, both languages should be assessed, as they can be complementary to each other – consider for example the vocabulary a child uses at home in the heritage language and that needed at school (or in the community).

Sequential bilinguals begin to learn the second language somewhat later than simultaneous bilinguals, usually when they enter school. Children with Specific Language Impairment (SLI) will need some years to catch up to monolinguals who are similarly affected. The same has been reported in typically developing children who also lag behind in second language development. This is not surprising, since learning a second language takes time. With regard to children with Down Syndrome (DS) or Autism Spectrum Disorder (ASD), "the current evidence shows no detrimental effects of sequential bilingualism if you take into account both languages of the bilingual child when making comparisons."

How can parents and practitioners best support children with AN in their life with two or more languages?

My tip for parents who raise their children with multiple languages, no matter if they have AN or not, is to observe them closely and avoid comparing them to other children. Every child develops in its own way – even overall development of siblings can differ considerably.

When parents have concerns about the development of their child, it is important for them to know what their child is able and comfortable to do in different settings being at home, outside of home, in different societal situations etc.. Parents should also be knowledgeable on what their child needs in order to be confident (for example in assessment situations). – These are important details parents will have to share with professionals who will assess their child.

When families get the advice that their children need additional support, a quest for solutions starts that seems never-ending. Online forums and chat groups, but also scientific research are where they gather information from. Both sources are important and valuable to find out what is possible and desirable from a research and personal point of view. I, personally, see the problem in the frustration that this may cause in some parents who observe that their children are not developing in the way other children do, or who realize that they don't find the kind of support and therapy others talk about.

Our expectations always depend on our experiences. When parents are trying to figure out what help they can get for their AN children, they assume that things are done similarly everywhere. I recommend not taking anything for granted, because what is common sense and practice in one country might not be in another one. Practices differ from country to country and it is fundamental to make a reality check in order to know what is possible and to be prepared and flexible with regard to possible solutions. This applies to the AN of the child as well as to the languages the child is learning.

Here is a list of some of the assumptions parents of children with AN usually make:

Assumption 1: Assessments are done early everywhere

Frequently, assessments start when the children join at daycare or preschool, wherein, depending on the country, the policies and the support systems in place, it will take months before the children get the help they need.

Families with AN children who live abroad, need to first find out what system is available. Dealing with different school systems and policies that are not as helpful and supportive as expected, as well as non-informed advice given by professionals is daunting: knowing that inclusion is not the norm everywhere will put you in the right mindset.

The underlying premise of inclusion is that all children can learn and belong to the mainstream of school and community life. Inclusion is a basic value that extends to all children (Dash, 2018): "There have always been children with diverse needs, but there have not always been educational programs to meet their needs."

When relocating repeatedly, you may prefer to consider staying longer in one place – or move earlier to another. Assessments and procedures require time and patience. Families who stay in one place for a shorter period might find going through the whole process over and over again too exhausting, not to mention the child, who would benefit from some continuity.

Fact is: Assessments are not done early and automatically everywhere. Inform yourself on early intervention programs in the area you live in or are moving to.

Assumption 2: Parents are supported to speak their heritage language with their children with AN

It seems obvious to maintain our heritage language with our children. Nevertheless, parents might still be advised to speak a language they are not fluent in with their children, although research proves that it has a negative impact on communication and connection with the children.

Interviews with parents of children with Autism Spectrum Disorder (ASD) show that parents feel less comfortable and less natural interacting with their child because of their discomfort. Needless to say that this has a detrimental effect on the child's language and overall development, especially on children with communication difficulties!

Even parents, who were comfortable speaking their non-heritage language with their children, expressed feelings of sadness and guilt for not passing on their language and culture. One also needs to consider the impact this has on the whole family, the siblings of the child, the extended family, etc. The sense of isolation and exclusion for a child with ASD or any other AN is immense because usually the rest of the family continues using the heritage language(s).

When children don't speak the same language as their parents or the rest of the family, they can't communicate with them! A mother (who wants to remain anonymous), told me during a consultation that when she was asked to speak a foreign language with her autistic daughter "it was like asking me to abandon my child", wherein the foreign language was the community language she barely understood (yet).

Without support of their families' heritage language, children may lose their ability to take part in family conversations, which can affect their relationships with family members, and they may lose or reject their ethnic identity. Additionally, parents may not have the ability to communicate in the majority language and thus cannot provide quality language models in that language. As a result, if the minority language is excluded from the intervention, parents may communicate less with their children and may participate in fewer cultural activities in their heritage language. Also, when children are not able to speak the heritage language, parents may feel a sense of sadness and loss, because language is a key component of one's cultural identity (De Houwer 2017).

Many AN children have learning difficulties. Active involvement in conversations is fundamental for language improvement – whenever possible and to the extent their disability allows them to do so of course. Language input and stimulation by two-way conversations has been proven to be positively related to language proficiency.

The quality of the interactions is more important than quantity. Children with developmental disabilities need to experience their languages in a functional and interactive way, designed to facilitate their language learning.

For autistic children, it is very important to speak the heritage language, since, "unlike normal children who learn the rules of speech acts and social functioning instinctually, (they) need to be exposed to a variety of social situations to learn the rules governing them" (Kremer-Sadlik, 2005: 1232). Therefore we should "not limit their access to conversations, and especially, to those that involve the autistic child's parents. For autistic children, their parents are their primary source for language input, imitation, and practice, whether the children actively engage in activities with the parents or simply overhear parents' social interactions" (Kremer-Sadlik, 2005: 1232).

Gonzalez Barrero 2017 and others have observed a "bilingual advantage in set-shifting skills as measured by an experimental task, to children with ASD (...) bilingualism is not harmful (...), and in fact, may provide some advantages, such as mitigating prominent set-shifting difficulties. (...) Bilingualism, under the right conditions, may act as a protective factor for certain EF difficulties for populations with neurodevelopmental disorders." This kind of findings emphasizes a bilingual advantage. As positive and encouraging as they are for everyone, like myself, who advocates for everyone's right to speak and learn their own languages, they should be taken with a grain of salt. There have been some objections about the methods used to achieve these results and more research needs to be done. – What one can take away from them though is that parents should keep speaking their heritage language with their AN children.

In this context, parents of children with and without AN should follow the advice of professionals who know about these studies and about how multilinguals acquire and learn languages, and what support is most suitable for them.

Fact is: Parents are still advised to prefer the community language (or school language, or language their children receive the treatment in) when they talk with their children.

Assumption 3: Multilingual children are assessed in all their languages

Intervention services for multilingual children with AN **should** be provided in all relevant languages for the child.

This might be possible in some cases and with some languages, but it is very unlikely that we can find professionals that are fluent or proficient in all our languages, everywhere.

"Multilingual children with PLI [Primary Language Impairment] benefit most from treatments designed to support all three key areas of development: L1, L2 and cognitive processing skills" (Ebert et al. 2014). Furthermore, they demonstrate impairment in both (or all) their languages and an effective intervention that involves both (or all) languages is essential "for improving language and, by extension, academic and social outcomes."

A study about the beliefs of Speech-Language Pathologists (SLP) during language assessments of bilingual and bicultural individuals, shows how difficult it is to find the right help for multilingual children. The study analyzed the challenge of appropriate assessment of communication differences and disorders of multilingual and multicultural individuals (children and adults). SLPs were required to "use an assessment process that reliably differentiates true language disorders from language differences." (Papoutsis Kritikos, 2003, 73)

Slightly more than half of the participants (52%) – monolingual SLPs as well as second language SPLs (who learned a second language via academic study) – reported that "bilingual input in a child's environment would influence their interpretation of that child's language assessment results."

Children with language disorders or other disabilities need to be able to use all means of communication and this involves all their languages. The skills they learn from one language can be transferable to the other. Multilingual children need all their languages in order to learn and communicate at home and school, as well as in the community (Bigelow & Collins 2019 and Garcia & Tupas 2019).

Fact is: Most assessments are done in the community language only.

Assumption 4: SLPs, therapists, etc. assess multilingual children in different settings, at school as well as at home

Social interactions at home provide opportunities for "absorbing the values of a culture, such as rules of politeness, story-telling conventions, gender roles, and other pragmatic influences on interaction" (Papoutsis Kritikos, 2003, 75). A SLP with an authentic bicultural experience has a greater understanding for a bilingual and bicultural client. ASHA states that there is a need for SLP who bring sensitivity to communication and cultural issues.

Although according to the ASHA guidelines, "bilingual and monolingual individuals should have an equal chance of receiving needed language therapy" (ASHA 1995), "almost 40% of the participants [of the aforementioned study by Papoutsis Kritikos 2003] reported that they would not be equally as likely to refer an individual with bilingual input for intervention as a child who hears only one language".

As a result of the study: "the most accurate, comprehensive, and culturally appropriate language assessment is useless if the interpretation and decision-making phase of the process is biased" (Papoutsis Kritikos, 2003, 85).

It appears that the degree of multilingualism and multiculturalism among practicing SLP has a considerable impact on the assessment. Although one would expect that the situation has changed since this study in 2003, and it certainly has in some countries, examples like Millie's (which is not an exception), show that we can not assume that our SLP (or other therapist), has the necessary experience with multilingual and multicultural families. If we want to be sure that our child receives the right assessment and that the decisions made about the therapy are not biased, we have to be informed about the process, work closely with the practitioners and be well informed about the options.

Fact is: It is not uncommon that children are assessed by a team that is unfamiliar with the heritage language and culture, and that the child is only assessed in one setting. Furthermore, children from multilingual environments may be falling through the cracks by being under-referred or over-referred.

Assumption 5: Children with AN have access to bilingual programmes and services

Unfortunately, this is not always the case. The studies in the 2016 Journal of Communication Disorders show that simultaneous and sequential bilinguals with disabilities "were taught only in the majority language and were assessed and treated only in that language more often than they should be." Unfortunately, the more severe the disability, the less likely children with developmental disabilities have access to bilingual support and services.

Elizabeth Kay-Raining Bird had a team interviewing practitioners and administrators to identify barriers that prevent children with developmental disabilities from accessing and/or participating fully in bilingual services and supports, and they found "both systemic barriers (e.g. limits in funding, service availability varying by geographic location, etc.) and barriers specific to children with developmental disabilities such as a tendency to prioritize special education services over bilingual services, a lack of integration of special education and bilingual services, and so on."

Fact is: For children with AN, access to bilingual programs and interventions is not the norm.

Assumption 6: The support given to children with AN at school or by therapist will be enough

This is one point that applies to all children with AN, no matter the issue they have.

Most parents aim for their children to become balanced multilinguals and preferably (nearly) native fluent in all their languages. It might come as a surprise, but this is already an unrealistic goal for many children who don't have AN. Raising a child with multiple languages requires consistent use and improvement in all the languages.

It is more realistic to define what languages our children with AN need in their daily life, to what extent – up to what level of fluency – and what they can achieve considering their very personal development in a short and long term. Furthermore, parents need to take an active role in this process and help their children deal with all their languages and foster their skills.

When defining goals, for the overall development and language learning of AN children, it is important to know the time and energy that can be put into this by the parents, as they must be actively involved in their children's language acquisition and learning process.

"Best practice for both children and adults dictates that individuals (as age permits) and their families participate in the setting of goals as well as in the planning and implementation of therapy." (De Houwer 2019: 384)

"It is critical that SLPs understand and incorporate the individuals' and families' beliefs about language, communication, and language disorders; styles of interaction; daily activities and who participates in those activities; and goals for therapy and the extent to which they want to be involved and who should be involved." (Hammer 1998)

Whenever a child needs support, it will require the parents' active involvement that can consist of homework given by the therapist. The problem is, that "some parents may not perform the activities at home, because the recommendation does not fit their beliefs and practices. To achieve congruence, SLPs may instead train older siblings to conduct the play activity and/or may look for language-intense times during the daily routine when parents spend time with their children and integrate the therapy targets into these naturally occurring activities." (Scheffner Hammer and Edmonds 2019: 385)

Fact is: Parental involvement is fundamental for the development of the child; siblings and other family members can take an active part too.

I cannot stress this enough: Parents play a fundamental role in the overall progress of their children! This doesn't only concern the AN but also the language goals.

Parents have unique knowledge and expertise about their childrens' abilities, interests, likes, dislikes, strengths, needs, routines and experiences. This is important information that can assist professionals (practitioners, teachers etc.) in meeting the needs and providing the necessary support. When parents and professionals form collaborative relationships, they give the children the best chance to develop, learn and thrive.

Sometimes it seems to be an uphill battle, like the one Millie fought. Parents of AN children need to become experts and advocates for their children. For some parents this is too much. This is why communities, online forums, readings etc. are necessary for support and encouragement.

Only when parents know what is possible and what are viable options for their children and themselves – including siblings! – can they seek the most suitable help and determine in extent, thus their village. Following an African saying and adjusting it to the topic of this chapter: We need a multilingual village of supportive people to raise a multilingual child with AN.

Once parents and practitioners define the attainable goals for the children, they can design a plan that will help them and everyone else in their village to reach them.

Especially families who move frequently want to make sure that the children – and the family – receive continuous support and they want transitions to be as smooth as possible.

The example of Millie, who knows about multilingualism and knows that speaking her own language to her son won't harm him, demonstrates that even if parents are well-informed and experts, they might have to constantly convince others about what is possible and should be done. A solid action plan, elaborated with knowledgeable practitioners will help the children and the family to find the most suitable solution.

Don't forget your plan B...

Not every family living abroad wants to consider this, or can afford this at any time, but when children with AN do not receive the expected and needed support in the country they live in, parents should always contemplate the option to move to a country where the children would receive the help they need.

For some families this means saying goodbye to a mobile life, returning to the country of origin or a country where they lived before.

I have seen several families take this decision for their child's sake. This is why families should regularly assess their situation and evaluate possible solutions when they are on an international journey.

To sum it up:

1) Determine the communicative needs of the children and the language(s) with which they must be familiar.

2) Consider the children's relative ability in the different languages and the willingness and ability of the family members and school personnel to function in the various languages, as well as the children's attitude toward language learning in general.

3) Discover what support is available in your area and if the heritage languages of your children are being considered (and to what extent).

4) Maintain your heritage language for emotional and behavioral regulation and for the family and cultural relatedness, which should be weighed against competing needs.

5) Find your village, i.e. people within your family and community who are actively involved in supporting your children, and experts who can guide you and outline a plan that considers the current research about the AN of your children and their languages.

6) Choose the education system that supports your children with their AN and their heritage languages, possibly with the help of a professional. Depending on the AN of your children, decide with experts about additional languages.

7) Provide optimal, intense and well-structured input in the languages the AN children must be familiar with. Consult with the professionals about tutoring, pedagogically designed natural language environments, language-rich activities etc. in all the languages your children need.

8) Be aware that you might have to re-adjust your priorities at any moment along the journey.

References

- (American Speech and Language Association (ASHA) 1995).

- ASHA: American Speech Language Hearing Association, 1995, Communication development and disorders in multicultural populations: Readings and related materials, Rockville, MD: Author.
- ASHA: Help finding a professional speech-language pathologists and audiologists
- Baker, Colin, 2011, Foundations of Bilingual Education and Bilingualism, Multilingual Matters.
- Bedore, Lisa, Kay-Raining Bird, Elizabeth, and Genesee, Fred (eds.). 2016, The road to bilingualism: Access, participation and support for children with developmental disabilities across contexts, Journal of Communication Disorders, 63, 1-92:
- Kay-Raining Bird, Elizabeth and Fred Genesee, Ludo Verhoeven, 2016, Bilingualism in children with developmental disorders: A narrative review, Journal of Communicative Disorders, 63, 1-14.
- Pesco, Diane and Andrea A.N. MacLeod, Elizabeth Kay-Raining Bird, Patricial Cleave, 2016, A multi-site review of policies affecting opportunities for children with developmental disabilities to become bilingual, Journal of Communication Disorders, 63, 15-31.
- De Valenzuela, Julia, and Elizabeth Kay-Raining Bird, Karisa Parkington, Pat Mirenda, Kate Cain, Andrea A.N. MacLeod, Eliane Segers, 2016, Access to opportunities for bilingualism for individuals with developmental disabilities: Key informant interviews, Journal of Communication Disorders, 63, 32-46.
- Stefka, H. Marinova-Todd, Paola Colozzo, Pat Mirenda, Hillary Stahl, Elizabeth Kay-Raining Bird, Karisa Parkington, Kate Cain, Julia Scherba de Valenzuela, Eliane Segers, Andrea A.N. MacLeod, Fred Genesee, Professional practices and opinions about services available to bilingual children with developmental disabilities: An international study, Journal of Communication Disorders, 63, 47-62.
- Kay-Raining Bird, Elizabeth, Natacha Trudeau, Ann Sutton, Pulling it all together: The road to lasting bilingualism for children with developmental disabilities, Journal of Communication Disorders, 63, 63-78.

- Paradis, Johannes, 2016, An agenda for knowledge-oriented research on bilingualism in children with developmental disorders, Journal of Communication Disorders, 63, 79-   84.
- Peña, Elizabeth D., 2018, Supporting the home language of bilingual children with developmental disabilities: From knowing to doing, Journal of Communication Disorders, 63, 85-92.
- Bedore, Lisa and Peña Elizabeth, 2008, Assessment of Bilingual Children for Identification of Language Impairment: Current Findings and Implications for Practice, International Journal of Bilingual Education and Bilingualism, 11:1, 1-29.
- Bigelow, Martha and Penelope Collins, 2019, Bilingualism from Childhood through Adolescence, in De Houwer, Annick and Lourdes Ortega (eds.), The Cambridge Handbook of Bilingualism, CUP, 36-58.
- Dash, Neena, 2018, Significance of multilingualism for children with diverse needs & benefits in inclusive education: a qualitative study, International Journal of Creative Research Thoughts,1428-1435.
- De Houwer, Annick and Lourdes Ortega, eds. 2019, The Cambridge Handbook of Bilingualism, CUP.
- De Houwer, Annick, 2017, Minority language parenting in Europe and children's well-being, in N. Cabrera & B. Leyendecker (eds.), Handbook on positive development of minority children and youth, Berlin: Springer, 231-246.
- Ebert, Kerry Danahy and Kathryn Kohnert, Giang Pham, Jill Rentmeester Disher, Bita Payesteh, 2014, Three Treatments for Bilingual Children With Primary Language Impairment: Examining Cross-Linguistic and Cross-Domain Effects, Journal of Speech, Language and Hearing Research, 57, 172-186.
- Garcia, Ofelia and Ruanni Tupas, 2019, Doing and Undoing Bilingualism in Education, in De Houwer, Annick and Lourdes Ortega (eds.), The Cambridge Handbook of Bilingualism, CUP, 390-407.
- Gonzalez-Barrero, Ana Maria, and Aparna S. Nadig, 2017, Verbal fluency in bilingual children with Autism Spectrum Disorders, Linguistic Approaches to Bilingualism, 7:13, 460-475.

- Gonzalez-Barrero, Ana Maria, and Aparna S. Nadig, 2017, Can Bilingualism Mitigate Set-Shifting Difficulties in Children With Autism Spectrum Disorders?, Child Development, 1-18.
- Gonzalez-Barrero, Ana Maria, and Aparna S. Nadig, 2018, Bilingual children with autism spectrum disorders: The impact of amount of language exposure on vocabulary and morphological skills at school age: Language skills in bilingual children with ASD, Autism Research, 11:12, 1667-1678.
- Grosjean, François, 2008, Studying Bilinguals, Oxford University Press.
- Grosjean, François, 2017, Supporting Bilingual Children With Special Education Needs. An interview with Elizabeth Kay-Raining Bird, posted January 18th 2017, https://www.psychologytoday.com.
- Hammer, C.S. 1998, Toward the "thick description" of families: Using ethnography to overcome the obstacles to providing family-centered early intervention services, American Journal of Speech-Language Pathology, 7:1, 5-22.
- Hårkansson, Gisela, 2017, Typological and developmental considerations on specific language impairment in monolingual and bilingual children: A Processability Theory account, Language Acquisition, 24:3, 265-280.
- Korkoman, Marit, Stenroos, Maria, Mickos, Annika, Westman, Martin, Ekholm, Pia, Byring, Roger, 2012, Does simultaneous bilingualism aggravate children's specific language problems?, in Acta Paediatrica, 101:9, 946-952.
- Kremer-Sadlik, Tamar, 2005, To Be or Not to Be Bilingual: Autistic Children from Multilingual Families, Proceedings of the 4th International Symposium on Bilingualism, ed. James Cohen, Kara T. McAlister, Kellie Rolstad, and Jeff MacSwan, Somerville, MA: Cascadilla Press, 1225-1234.
- Papoutsis Kritikos, Effie, 2003, Speech-Language Pathologists' Beliefs About Language Assessment of Bilingual/Bicultural Individuals, Journal of Speech-Language Pathology, 12, 73-91.

- Romaine, Suzanne, 2006, The bilingual and multilingual community, in Tej K. Bhatia & William C. Ritchie (eds.), The Handbook of Bilingualism, Malden, MA: Blackwell Publishing.
- Scheffner Hammer, Carol and Lisa A. Edmonds, Bilingualism in Clinical Linguisticsl, in De Houwer, Annick and Lourdes Ortega (eds.), The Cambridge Handbook of Bilingualism, CUP, 369-389.
- Toppelberg, Claudio, Snow, Catherine, Tager-Flusberg, Helen, 1999, Severe Developmental Disorders and Bilingualism, Journal of the American Academy of Child and Adolescent Psychiatry, 38:9, 1197-1199.

Confident moms raise confident kids - On finding your tribe abroad

by Lisa Ferland

"Please let him get the job, please let him get the job, please let him get the job," I kneeled on the floor of my bedroom in Atlanta, Georgia and prayed. I rarely prayed for anything. I once prayed for my mom during her heart surgery, and He pulled through for me. This time, my conversation with God was quite different. I was begging to give birth to a new future—one that I desperately wanted to bring to fruition.

Our problems at home were mounting, and this job opportunity in Sweden seemed like the escape route we needed. A life raft with a rope that would drag us from the deep south to the great north. Our lives in Atlanta, USA, looked wonderful on paper. We both had thriving careers, had two generous incomes, and just produced a rosy-cheeked baby boy. Our family was growing, and things felt right.

It looked like I was going to have to accept the fact that my husband's consulting job made him work until 2 am some mornings. That was the nature of things. I also had to accept that the woman we hired to watch our son often fell asleep while he napped. "That's ok. I do that too," I thought. Except she wasn't me, and I wasn't the one napping with my baby while he slept during the day. I was in an office, hooked up to a machine pumping breast milk during conference calls, pretending I didn't feel like a cow. My milk supply was dropping due to this stupid artificial pump. It wouldn't be long before we'd stop our breastfeeding journey altogether.

At home, I watched the jogging stroller moms race to the lush green Piedmont Park down the street. They'd bundle up their babies against the chilly October morning and workout in the park at 5 am. The strollers folded expertly into their oversized SUVs and they'd drop their kids off at daycare on the way to work. These were my people. Were these my people?

Our son did not sleep through the night for months. He was six months old when my manager said, "You know, he really is capable of sleeping through the night by now." Yeah, but he wasn't and I was up every two hours while my husband traveled across the country for work. One night, my husband opened the front door, and I shoved our son into his arms. I walked past him into the night, down the street, and bought myself a night of quiet in a hotel in the city. Our situation wasn't working anymore, and something needed to change.

A job opportunity arrived at my husband's work inbox—a job opportunity in Sweden. Sweden! The land with long parental leaves, feminism, subsidized childcare, and socialized healthcare. It sounded too good to be true. We grasped at the opportunity as if we were drowning in our own ambition. "Should I apply? It's in Sweden. We've never been to Sweden..." my husband said. "Yes! Oh my God, yes!"

The fantasies of living and raising our family in Sweden filled my head and became the only thing I could imagine. I envisioned a life with parental leave benefits; this myth called a "work-life balance," and the chance to raise our kids in multiple languages. We would be so cultured, so experienced, and so much healthier than we were. I didn't realize that all adventures come at a price. For me, that price was my career.

At the time, I paid it willingly. Gladly, even. I was so happy to finally spend time at home with my child—the child whose growth and development milestones I had missed while I worked at a job with zero chance for upward movement. In our tiny Stockholm rental apartment, I held my son in my arms and asked him, "What are we going to do today?" I asked him because I had no idea. We were alone together in a foreign city while Daddy went to work all day. It was time for me to find a new tribe.

The effort required to build a community of friends who love you as much as your family loves you is herculean. It can feel impossible at times when you go on a seemingly never ending string of blind friendship dates with other parents.

"Let's exchange phone numbers so we can meet up for a coffee," a beautiful Italian woman with dark hair juggled her 10-month-old son on her lap. We had just finished a stroller walk with a large group, and four of us needed more than just an hour of strolling. We found a "stroller cafe"—a coffee house with twelve strollers parked out front on the Stockholm street and a cacophony of baby and toddler noise on the inside. Mothers tried to carry on coherent conversations over the sounds of children babbling, the banging noise of plastic toys on tables, and the whistling sounds of steamed milk for cappuccinos. The baristas of the cafe were both grateful and annoyed to have their workplace dominated by this loud group of parents on extended parental leave.

Around every table, I saw women expertly balancing their children and their social needs. They bounced babies on one knee and sipped their coffees off to the side. The lucky mothers had babies napping in their strollers outside the cafe. They drank their coffee in relative peace, and they sat differently than the rest—relaxed.

"We could get together again for a stroller walk. My son wakes up as soon as I bring him inside. He'll only sleep while I'm walking," the Italian woman continued. Our International Mothers Stroller Walk Meet-Up was like the United Nations but with strollers and talk of sleepless nights. There was a Canadian woman, two Australians who walked together, me, the American, and this Italian woman who kept proposing a future, more personal get together.

A mom date, of sorts.

We exchanged numbers, and I made sure to always meet up with her when she texted me. We had many coffee dates after that initial meeting and soon, she invited me to dinner. A night out with friends? Was it possible? We moved to Sweden with zero network, zero local language skills, and no idea what Stockholm city life entailed. Of course, I said yes.

I went to dinner that night only knowing one person. Luckily for me, she knew three other very nice women. We all had children around the same age. We laughed, we talked about illicit topics (like postpartum sex and all of the things I never dared share with anyone else). I stepped out of my comfort zone and shared beyond. I listened hard. I cared.

We had such a great time that we vowed to meet up again next month. Each dinner was a magical night out into the sexy world of Stockholm. For one night every six weeks or so, I didn't trudge behind a stroller, sling a diaper bag, or worry about a baby crying right as I started to enjoy my meal.

Those nights out were necessary for my sanity. They were crucial to making me feel like an adult again. For that night, I could think of myself. Those nights felt wonderfully selfish.

I needed only a small dose of selfishness to balance out the rest. The rest of the month, I served as our family's logistics coordinator, laundry flipper and folder, toddler wrangler, cultural integration manager, friend finder, translator, grocery decoder, and all of the little tasks that felt monumental when forced to be done in a foreign language and culture.

Building a community of peers who understood what it was like to stand in my shoes was essential. They served as a barometer of what "normal" was when nothing felt normal. They reassured me that their child was also struggling with X, Y, and Z, and not to worry about it. They acted as my safe space for venting about our beautiful, and incredible international opportunity that while fantastic, was also fraying my last nerve.

You're going to have to date around

When looking for your tribe—your people who get you no matter what—you're going to have to kiss a lot of frogs to find them.

When looking for your tribe, don't get hung up on where everyone is from. You might discover that you have very little in common with people from your home country and more in common with other people. Try to connect with people on similarities in family values rather than citizenship.

When looking for your tribe, be adventurous and open-minded. Put yourself out there again and again. Don't be afraid to look like an idiot or say something stupid—you will probably do both. Have a sense of humor and forgive yourself.

When looking for your tribe, try to make local friends—people who aren't on assignment and who won't be leaving anytime soon. These people serve as anchors and can be those people who have historical knowledge as to why things are the way they are.

When looking for your tribe, remember to be you. You have been gifted with a clean slate. With every move, every new location, you get to be whoever you want to be. Choose to be kind, open, and giving, and your community will react in kind.

It's been over seven years since our first coffee date, and now that Italian woman who asked to exchange phone numbers is my daughter's godmother. We live only 20 minutes apart by car, and we have a permanent space in each other's lives. May the friendships you keep be the ones worth fighting for.

One night after a dinner out with my friends, my homeward bound train pulled into the station at 10:45 pm. I looked over at the train car heading in the opposite direction toward the city to see two young women giggling together. They bent their heads toward one another, snapped a bright flash, and took a selfie with their phone. They were heading out on the town as I was heading home. Oh, how my nights had changed! Their train pulled away and took the specter of our carefree night along with it. I climbed into my warm bed that night ready for an early morning with my toddler thinking about how different and how wonderful life can be.

Media influences on children

by Dr. Brigitte Vittrup

Children these days spend a lot of time with various forms of screen media, including television, computers, websites, video games, and cell phones. Research shows that children in industrialized nations spend upwards of 6-8 hours per day engaged with screen media. This is despite the fact that various medical and scientific communities advise against excessive media use. For example, the American Academy of Pediatrics has for a long time recommended that children ages 2-17 spend no more than 2 hours per day in front of screens and that children under 2 have no screen time exposure. In addition, a recent consensus statement by the European Academy of Paediatrics and the European Childhood Obesity Group recommended a limit of 90 minutes per day due to the link between increased screen time and childhood obesity.

Decades of research have shown us that media exposure influences children's behavior, attitudes, and general development. Electronic media can sometimes be seen as a "window on the world." With the amount of time children spend in front of screens, they gain a lot of information – some of it true and realistic, and some of it not so much – about the world and the society they live in. Children who spend a lot of time with television, video games, and internet content are likely to think that at least a good amount of that content is a true representation of reality. Therefore, what they see is likely to influence them, because this content provides examples of behaviors, and the media characters can be seen as role models (both positive and negative). Over time, they may begin to imitate behaviors and pick up on various social attitudes about others (parents, authority figures, minority groups, etc.).

a) Positive influences of media

Electronic media offers a wealth of educational resources that can teach children from preschool through the teenage years important knowledge and skills. This includes educational websites that teach children language, reading, math, art, problem-solving, and social studies; video tutorials teaching children how to create things, build things, solve maths and statistical problems, and speak a foreign language; educational video games that can teach children problem-solving and spatial skills; and a variety of educational and informational television programs that can teach children all of the above. In addition, some programs can inspire pro-social learning, such as cooperation, helping behaviors, empathy, and moral values.

While there are a lot of positive educational resources available, they are not always the ones that are advertised most prominently, and therefore parents may need to help their children seek out these sites and programs. In addition, even positive media should be limited to a few hours per day.

b) Negative influences of media

Unfortunately, there is also a lot of negative content in electronic media. Over the past 50 years, violence in television, film, and video games has increased exponentially. In addition, live fight videos are being distributed on social media and video sharing websites, making them easily accessible to children. Research shows that frequent exposure to media violence can make children more aggressive because they learn that violence is a means to solve a problem. It can also make children more anxious and afraid because they learn that the world around them may be dangerous.

The amount of sexual content has also increased, and there is evidence that repeated exposure may lead to teenagers engaging in risky sexual behaviors at earlier ages.

Television and video games often portray minority populations in stereotyped and negative manners. For example, people of color are frequently portrayed as villains or criminals whereas white people are portrayed as being powerful and in leadership roles. Women are often objectified or portrayed as passive and less intelligent. Muslims are often portrayed as terrorists.

For children and youth belonging to marginalised groups, these portrayals can affect their self-esteem, aspirations for the future, and general vulnerability.

Finally, the increasing popularity of social media sites and the ability to connect with people worldwide through social media, internet groups, and video games, can leave children vulnerable to negative exposures, risky propositions, and bullying.

c) What parents can do

When children are young, parents have a lot of control over their children's access to media, and it is important to establish good rules and habits early on. However, research from both Europe and the United States shows that many parents are unaware of their children's media habits and do not enforce many media rules at home. There are various rules parents can put in place to selectively restrict the amount of time children spend with electronic media (for example, no more than 2 hours per day), the content they are allowed to access (based on their age), and the context of the media exposure (for example, watching TV with the children, having a computer or video game console in a family room instead of the child's bedroom, and not allowing them to interact with unknown individuals online).

Even with established media rules, children may at times – either deliberately or accidentally – be exposed to inappropriate content. Therefore, it is important that parents discuss the content, help children understand what is appropriate/inappropriate and why, and help them develop media literacy skills. Young children, due to cognitive limitations, do not yet have the ability to critically evaluate the content they are exposed to, such as intent, purpose, persuasion, and depictions of so-called reality. By discussing these, parents can help children develop these skills. Being able to critically evaluate media content can help buffer any negative effects of media exposure. Critically evaluating content includes identifying what is appropriate and inappropriate, as well as understanding that information may be biased or slanted, and that not everything you read on websites or see on television is the unbiased truth. In addition, parents should help their children seek out positive content that can help educate them and inspire positive self-esteem.

It is still important to remember that even positive content and educational media cannot replace direct interaction with positive role models. Children can often learn more from conversations and engaging activities with family members and peers. One of the reasons for the advised restrictions on screen time for very young children is that children need direct face-to-face interactions with others for proper brain development in the early years. Children's cognitive development is aided by the bidirectional interactions with more knowledgeable others, such as adults, and their developing social skills benefit from direct interactions and feedback from peers and adults.

The more time children spend with media, the less time they spend in social interactions with others, and therefore it is important to limit their exposure to the extent possible. However, given the easy access and a wealth of media technologies available to children, the reality is that they will continue to spend a lot of time with electronic media. In addition, media content is not likely to become more child-friendly. But the influence of media on children's behavior, attitudes, and development can be mediated by the context in which the exposure occurs. Thus, the onus is on parents to be involved in their children's media use by monitoring, selectively restricting, and discussing the media content with their children.

The impact of culture on the education of the young

by Brian Vassallo

The political history, life outlook and cultural milieu of particular groups of children impact heavily upon the values and expectations placed on the children themselves. It is vital for educators, along the course of their experience in working with children, to garner knowledge of the cultural patterns in the community of the students with whom they interact.

These differences may cause educators to inaccurately judge students from some cultures as poorly behaved or disrespectful. In addition, because cultural differences are hard to perceive, students may find themselves reprimanded by educators but fail to understand what they did that caused concern. Take for example the students who collaborate with peers on a task. At first glance, it might seem that nothing is inappropriate, but when helping is extended to writing of assignments or the involvement of families in composing the assignment then helping might be perceived as cheating rather than guiding. Also, if a teacher expects his/her class to be arguing around a presented topic, then those students who are quiet might be thought of as being disrespectful or lazy. Also, conflicts might arise in cases where students are brought up in environments where the property is communal but then are taught in environments where a high degree of individuality and self-achievement is encouraged.

The influence of culture, on anything that surrounds education, has a direct influence on students' participation style. Both in Europe and in the USA, students are thought to be proactive in their learning experiences, value classroom discussions and look at teachers in the eye as a sign of respect. On the other hand, Asian students, especially females, are encouraged to exhibit low profiles and eye-contact with teachers is considered to be rather offensive.

Also, some parents from Latin America tend to view teachers as experts and highly regard their opinion when it comes to important decisions on the future of their children's academic careers. In contrast, however, most European and American parents adopt a more continuous involvement in their children's career paths, consult teachers on an ad hoc basis but finally decide on their own accord together with their children.

These cultural underpinnings have a direct bearing on the perceptions which educators have on American, European and Asian parents. Keeping in mind that different cultural groups adopt different interaction patterns, language prosodics and demeanor is of paramount importance. When educators become cognizant of the panacea of cultural differences within and across cultural groups they start realizing that successful schooling is the result of a multitude of constructs that need to take into account the students' cultural makeup.

Educators need to be careful not to push personal cultural patterns upon students which counter the values and traditions ingrained in the cultural makeup of the students under their care. Being respectful as to what is positive and ethical in various cultural systems should be the hallmark in all educational systems. Negative or disrespectful mechanisms that undermine or diminish the human respect of the "other" should be addressed in a way that increases the cultural richness of all those concerned.

a) Children's behaviors and cultural factors

It must be stated from the outset that neither families nor schools can provide an answer for children's behaviors. Parents, teachers, and children are themselves a product of an encompassing culture, which transforms itself with the changing times, promises new value sets, behavioral standards, and expectations. Children's behaviors are the reflection of what adults present to them as the 'appropriate' culture to live in. When these expected behaviors, the ones proposed by the school and the ones brought about by the home environment, are in conflict with one another then problems are bound to occur. Different cultural forces play their part in pushing and pulling our children in one direction and not in another with the undesirable effect of labeling a child as 'culturally deviant' depending as to whether s/he is at home or at school.

Other forces that are likely to bring about tension in children's expected behaviors include adherence to community standards, influence by the media, mixed marriages, changing attitudes to sexuality and other factors. All these come into play when examining children's behaviors.

b) Community standards

Community standards (especially those associated with minor communities) are frequently in dissonance with mainstream standards. Examples include attire, teen socialization, sexual encounters, dating, and others. Children and teenagers are frequently 'torn apart' between having to conform to the norms transcended to them by their families and those of the society in which they reside. Children and teenagers who practice particular religious teachings may be excluded, stigmatized and ostracised by their peers while on the other hand, those who do not conform to their religious obligations are haunted with feelings of extreme guilt and in danger of eventual community exclusion.

c) The Media

Media affects children's behavior and debating their influence in this book can be a laborious task. It is clear, however, that behavioral expectancies depicted in the media are not consonant with some community expectancies. For example, newspapers and magazines advertise clothing which is dissonant to some cultures. They use peer pressure techniques, influencing children into purchasing an expensive mobile phone and not a cheaper brand. This puts undesirable pressure on families of low economic backgrounds. This provides fertile ground for conflicts and discord in families. Similar examples include clothing, entertainment, and leisure activities.

d) Mixed marriages

Children coming from mixed marriages may have a hard time developing a sense of identity, especially during adolescence. They experience difficulty in affirming their uniqueness while recognizing the positive impact which both cultures had in their upbringing. Harnessing this positivity and using it in critical moments in their life is of vital importance.

e) Changing attitudes to Sexuality

Adolescents today have to contend between the freedom which society glorifies and the responsibility which educators promote at every opportunity. Children and adolescents are frequently at crossroads between the cultural values inculcated earlier and the emerging values of the digital age. Society presents adolescents with freedoms they are not equipped to handle, falls short equipping them with skills when they face challenges, yet castigates them for behaving irresponsibly.

Besides these factors, the children's self-esteem and their perception of how others see them have an influence on how they function at school and outside school. The way children evaluate and the way they react towards what happens around them is not culture-free.

f) Some suggestions

Hence it is important for parents and teachers to help children express their emotions and to speak up for their rights when the need arises. Show openness to your child's questions and teach them about anything in which they show interest. Allow your children to meet other children - both of a similar and of different ethnic background. This will boost their self-image and self-confidence. Also, encourage alternatives to clothing, food, music, and overall atmosphere, both at home and at school. For the very young ones, you can invest in multicultural toys, books and internet resources. You may also want to participate in multicultural events such as festivals, weddings, talent shows, etc. Help children understand that respect is common for all cultures.

Educating our younger society members is a rather complex, not to say an arduous task. The cultural makeup with which children are endowed since their very early years, and how it is developed as the years progress, is a subject of intense study and deep reflection. Care needs to be exercised to utilize children's cultural baggage as a tool towards more successful school and societal engagement.

Promoting Tolerance, practical tips - What we should do to enhance religious tolerance at home (parents) and at school (teachers)

by Brian Vassallo

"The highest result of education is tolerance." - Helen Keller

Religious tolerance: Why is it necessary?

It is actually quite hard to imagine a world with no or little religious tolerance. Given the rapid increase in globalisation, tolerance is a necessary prerequisite for society members to build relationships. The multiple variety of cultures and people with different religious beliefs, coexisting in an intermeshed network of social communication, seems to be the hallmark of the 21st century. When religious tolerance is established and practised consistently, unity and peaceful coexistence thrive among society members.

According to the website Tolerance.org, a hate crime is committed every hour, 50% of which are committed by young men in their late teens. Furthermore, The

Leadership Conference Education Fund states that religious and racial biases are developed during early childhood and are fertile ground for numerous stereotypes by the time a child is twelve years of age.

The need for more religious tolerance seems to come in synchrony with the compelling necessity to celebrate differences and heterogeneity. Henry Giroux, an American and Canadian scholar and cultural critic, further clarifies that, when emphasising difference and pluralism, a new and dynamic experience is created which ushers us into "hear(ing) the voices of others". It is in such particular snapshots in time and frequently unpredictable moments, that we are frequently called to fulfil the noble mission of transmitting tolerant attitudes to those around us. It is also quite difficult to determine the effects that these debates have on the younger generation. As parents and educators, it is our responsibility to stimulate and support healthy discussions within our families and schools but also to prevent destructive patterns possibly stemming from emotional turmoil, arising from these debates.

Teaching religious tolerance at home

The home environment is the ideal place to teach children about religious tolerance. Primarily we need to examine our embedded beliefs and attitudes toward those who profess a different faith than ours. Such examination is crucial if we are to encourage our children to be critical and equip them with the necessary skills to detect even the slightest of stereotypical messages and discriminatory practices. It is a certainty that the prevalent attitudes cultivated in the home environment have the greatest impact on the way children perceive those who are different. For a start it would be ideal to discuss with your child how you came to believe in what you profess to believe. This sharing of information is crucial as it provides the children with an understanding of the background for adhering to particular sets of religious beliefs and not others.

It is also crucial to instil in your child the love of learning and the love of reading. Reading with your child about different world religions is not only a shared pleasurable experience but sets the ground for respecting diversity and mutual tolerance. Engage in open discussions, highlight similarities and differences whilst keeping a positive outlook. When engaging in discussions, stress the importance of religious freedom among your family members as well as for others, making sure that your child understands the difference between accepting the person and adopting his/her religious beliefs.

Take pride in urging your child to share his/her beliefs among friends and relatives whilst urging others to reciprocate by sharing what they believe with your family. If you are concerned that your child might feel ostracised because of his/her expressed views, then discuss these feelings with the group/family member concerned and assume an active role in shaping the discussion to take an unbiased flow. Your child will notice your active role, internalize the positive attitude and unconsciously improve his/her skills at dealing with possible lack of self-worth. This will also help your child forge his/her way towards full acceptance within the immediate and extended society s/he lives in.

It would be opportune to encourage children to actively fight stereotypes and intolerant attitudes by those around them. This can be done by involving them in activities which promote diversity, tolerance and understanding. Such activities might include sports, art competitions, drama series or television quizzes. Engaging in these activities will give them an opportunity to express themselves in front of other children and take the opportunity to share their beliefs within a social atmosphere.

Direct confrontation is to be avoided and tactfully redirected in a more socially acceptable manner. This skill is not easy to master, especially for young children. But every instance of confrontation or harsh disagreement is simply another opportunity to further sharpen and widen an already existing repertoire of skills.

Finally, if your child attends after school religious activities, such as catechism lessons or Friday Salaat prayers, speak to the group leaders or educators to gauge prevalent attitudes of respect and tolerance. While, as a general rule, religious leaders are open to religious differences among community members, some may inadvertently perpetuate intolerance through inappropriate actions, insensitive speeches or poor use of language. As explained before, the effects are difficult to determine or to measure. If such incidences happen, it would be opportune for you, as a parent, to look into another church group or denomination which is more compatible with your world views, while at the same time not holding biases towards other groups. Similarly, as iterated above, be prepared to speak to the religious leaders and seek to establish ways and means on how to promote tolerance and mutual respect.

Schools: The place to tackle intolerant attitudes

Schools are not only a place to learn the three Rs – Reading, wRiting and aRithmetic, but an increasing need is felt to add another R- Relationships. School is not just a place to learn literacy and numeracy skills but is also a community building place where a large number of social activities take place. Schools, just like any other workplace, have policies which delineate rules that govern interpersonal relationships and behaviors. Carefully research the implications of those policies and the possible effects, positive or negative, which they might have on children's developing attitudes and behaviors. Undergo additional research to supplement your existing repertoire of knowledge and skills. Together with the school authorities, re-examine those policies in the light of what you have recently researched and purposefully use those rules to challenge underlying assumptions about tolerance. Use those policies to stimulate discussions around tolerance and increased respect.

At school, it is of utmost importance that textbooks and curricula are consonant with the principles and tenets of multicultural education, thus promoting equality, social justice and religious tolerance. Hence, do not be afraid to suggest alternative books from the ones children already have. Also, do not be afraid or intimidated to ask your child's educators about the methods they use to approach multiculturalism and equality teaching in their daily practice. Parents are important stakeholders in the educational process of their children. Probe into how teachers teach tolerance in their classroom. Delve in detail into what the vision of the school is and how and in what way this is translated towards tolerance and respect for others. If the school lacks the impetus towards diversity and tolerance education, transform yourself into a catalyst towards promoting change. Come up with a small project, promote it, clearly stating the positive outcomes arising from it. Try to work as a group, joining forces between teachers and parents, and come up with a proper motto such as "Together we achieve more".

As a parent you have every right to ensure that the school you send your child to promotes an environment that encourages empathy, compassion, respect, understanding and a sense of openness. You might consider initiating campaigns against bullying, name-calling, racism, intolerance and the subtle bigotry that stealthily hovers around school corridors.

Peer pressure is a tool which can work in our favour or against us. So, being able to use peer pressure to teach about the harm done by unfair behavior, social isolation and racist attitudes, is both a challenge and a skill.

Teacher bias

This is a difficult one! It's really hard to admit that those people who have dedicated a significant part of their lives, devoted their time and effort, and invested so much money in their profession, can themselves be biased. However, even the most keen and well-meaning teacher holds stereotypes and beliefs that inadvertently affect their students.

A nineteen-year-old belonging to a Jewish community said "One day in a Biology lecture we were bargaining with the lecturer not to give us an exam the next day. I happened to have one euro in my pocket and said, "I'll give you one euro if you forego the exam tomorrow." Another student from the back said "One euro is a lot of money to a Jew." The teacher brushed aside the comment, but later he pulled aside the young man who told him that he was offended by the other student's comment. He politely commented that as a teacher, he could have done something more.

Personally, I think that the teacher should have stopped the lesson and debated the statement of the student. The biology lesson could have continued with interesting parallelisms between natural diversity and socio-economic diversity. The teacher could have explained that while biological diversity is partly genetic and partly environmental, human diversity can also be a result of multiple factors – some of which are easily identifiable while others are not. The teacher could have brainstormed for such factors with all the students in class and also reflected on the impact which such factors had or could have had on the current socio-economic dynamics of families. This would also have prompted students to reflect on how they can assist others to reach more socioeconomic equity within a classroom environment.

Some thoughts on bullying

Bullying can be the result of religious intolerance and is manifested by various kinds of aggressive behavior. It is also characterised by a real or perceived imbalance of power. Both children and adults who have been bullied experience long term problems. Thus it is imperative to stop bullying at its very early stages. Bullying can take the form of physical force or use of personal information to create embarrassment and therefore controlling the person involved. It can also include threats, spreading rumours, physically or verbally attacking someone or deliberate exclusion from a group.

Refer to the school values

There are different ways to respond to bullying arising from religious affiliations. One of them is to assert one's own religious identity by voicing it out, and respond positively to it, for example "I feel great the way I practise my religion, what about you?". It always helps if you are surrounded with people who might help you. A network of support works wonders. Like the previous examples look into the anti-bullying policies of your school and see if you can mirror the situation you or your child might be in with the existing school policies. Is your school aware of anti-bullying or anti-harassment policies? Does your school have them? If not, start lobbying for such practices to come into place.

Also, refer to the school's mission (or vision) statement to challenge perpetuated inequities you see (or perceive) in your school. Politely but firmly draw the attention of the school administration, saying "This school is dedicated to providing every student with equity schooling and opportunities in a safe and healthy environment. How can we respect every religious denomination in our school?". Also, don't present yourself as an armchair critic! Be proactive and propose tangible realistic ideas together with a strong sense of reaching out. Offer assistance when you see others struggling for whatever reason.

Conclusion

Lack of religious tolerance is always a result of fear and insecurity. When we're scared of the unknown and start losing our locus of control, we usually attempt to annihilate that which is causing us to be unstable. So, my final advice towards raising tolerant multicultural children, is to work towards building confidence in them. Openness, self-respect, love, praise, positive criticism, honesty and realistic expectations are the keys necessary to bolster children's self-esteem and help to make them more secure and tolerant people, now and in the future.

Crossing the Deep Cultural Divide

by Tamara Yousry

"...whereas most Americans are repulsed by an Indonesian who blows his nose onto the street, the Indonesian is repulsed by the American who blows his nose in a handkerchief and then carries it around for the rest of the day in his pocket," (Ferraro, 2002).

Cliché as it sounds, the world is getting smaller. Whereas sixty years ago, flying to foreign lands was an activity reserved for the wealthy, educated and elite, today airports are full of sojourners from all walks of life making their way from one country to another to work, live and settle. Arabs are in Australia, the English are in Spain, Americans in Egypt, Mexicans in America and the Chinese in England. The list goes on and monocultural groups and teams are becoming a thing of the past.

In today's contemporary, globalised world, multicultural groups are the norm, people are global-trotting like there is no tomorrow, cultures are inter-marrying at staggering rates, even bringing to light the concept of "inter-faith" within these contexts, causing the world to appear smaller, as it becomes a melting pot of mix-matched folk. Yet, with all of these crossovers, misunderstandings are bountiful and breakdowns in communication inevitable, leading to bad feeling, confusion, collisions and frustration. Why is this so? And how can it be curbed?

What many sojourners who set forth on a new adventure to foreign lands fail to realise is that there are dozens upon dozens of cultural factors, most of them hidden, which, unless pointed out, inevitably become the fuel to set off potential fires of conflict and miscommunication. Not only are there obvious differences such as language barriers, dress styles or taste in food, but other small, less obvious factors, such as perceptions of authority and non-verbal communication, can also act as barriers, which can have many effects ranging from the prevention of successful integration into a new culture or the signing of a business deal.

One of the most helpful contributions to understanding why intercultural breakdowns occur is the "Iceberg metaphor" (https://www.researchgate.net/figure/An-iceberg-metaphor-for-culture_fig6_2993893 62). It is not certain who initially came up with it, however it is widely used today in intercultural contexts and classrooms to help explain the cultural intricacies behind our behavior. Most people have no idea that there is much, much more to an iceberg than meets the eye. In fact, when one looks at an iceberg, the part that is visible accounts for approximately ten percent of the entire creation. The other ninety percent is beneath the surface of the water, but, at best, we never think about this. At worst, we don't even know it.

The surface parts account for the things we are taught and are consciously aware of. For example: how to prepare food, folkloric traditions, literature, history, language, manners, customs and how people dress. In stark contrast are the cultural aspects we are less aware of, which we were not directly taught, but which, astoundingly, make up the majority of the equation. Some examples are: communication styles, role expectations, non-verbal communication, our patterns of interpersonal relationships, work and learning styles, what motivates us, our attitudes towards commitments and authority, negotiation styles and how we perceive professionalism. These "cultural makeup" aspects lie beneath the surface in the depths of our unconscious and are underpinned by our judgments, habits, attitudes, assumptions, understandings, values and perceptions. These factors are far more complicated to understand and analyse, as most of us do not know how, when and why they were formed.

Two other important components that aid in intercultural miscommunication are ethno-centricism and stereotyping. The former is the view that "my way is the right way" and the "exaggerated tendency to think the characteristics of one's own culture are central and superior to all other cultures, (Alan Cornes, 2004). The latter (stereotyping) is the process of categorising people, groups and cultures into tiny boxes and compartments in order to make sense of the world. For example, when someone meets a person from Country X, they immediately use the attributes they know about this culture and automatically stick this person in that specific category. Both of these concepts are detrimental in a cross-cultural environment.

It is interesting to look at several cultural dimensions that exist today, as they help to explain the different values different people inhibit. After all, the very fact that values are ranked and prioritised differently is the exact reason behind the profound contrast in behavior exhibited by people from different cultures.

Hofstede's Cultural Dimensions

"When somebody says privacy, I think of loneliness." - (Ethiopian student), Storti, 1999.

Individualism vs Collectivism:

Individualist cultures, such as the UK and USA, prioritise the self, or "I", while Collectivist cultures, such as Egypt, Spain and Brazil, prioritise "we", and have the interest of the whole group at heart. Individualist cultures tend to be more task-oriented, preferring to 'get the job done' as quickly as possible. Privacy is also highly valued. In organisations, employees are joined by a contract and their involvement is more contractual than moral.

In collectivist cultures, on the other hand, people tend to identify more with the group they are part of and people belong to extended families and clans who are there to offer protection and support in return for loyalty. The line between business and pleasure is more blurred and much time and energy is spent in investing in relationships with others. Harmony and cohesiveness is important and often takes precedence over individual opinions and concerns.

Low Power Distance Vs High Power Distance:

"The hierarchical nature of Indian society demands that there is a boss and that the boss should be seen to be the boss. Everyone else just does as they are told, and even if they know the boss is 100% wrong, no one will argue." - Gitanjali Kolanad, Culture Shock: India, (Storti, 1999).

Where the power lies, whether in the workplace, in the home, or in the classroom, varies from culture to culture and can overall resemble a small-scale political system. In egalitarian cultures, ones with 'small power distance' such as Sweden, the UK and USA, the workplace slightly resembles a democracy whereby power is decentralised and diffused to many people, social relations are informal, the salary range between the top and bottom of the organisation is narrow, manual work is no different in status than office work, subordinates expect to be (and are often) consulted and "the ideal boss is a resourceful democrat," (Hofstede & Hofstede, 2005). In short, if drawn, this pyramid is a low, flat one in which little distance between levels can be marked.

In hierarchical societies (who tend to be collectivist) such as Malaysia, Japan, China and Egypt, organisations reflect 'existential inequality' between people of different levels and positions. Power is centralised to only a few, superiors are not to be questioned, subordinates expect to be told what to do, the salary range between people of high low positions is wide and "the ideal boss is a benevolent autocrat or 'good father,'" (Hofstede & Hofstede, 2005). This pyramid tends to be much taller and narrower.

Masculine (Tough) Vs Feminine (Tender):

"Maintaining a peaceful, comfortable atmosphere is more important (to Koreans) than attaining immediate goals or telling the absolute truth." - Sonja Vegdahl Hur & Ben Seunghwa Hur, Culture Shock: Korea, (Storti, 1999).

This dimension has to do with how a culture defines success. A masculine culture defines success according to masculine traits such as achievement, assertiveness, power, competition and material accumulation. A feminine culture defines success based on its nurturing, social relationships, cooperation and opportunities for spiritual growth, (Ferraro, 2002). To elaborate, masculine cultures are more likely to restrict certain roles to certain genders, whereas in feminine cultures, such as Scandinavian ones, this would not be the case.

Fons Trompenaars and Charles Hampden-Turner's Cultural Dimensions

Neutral Vs Emotional:

"Egyptians will put their pride before their interest. If they feel insulted or patronised, they would rather take their business elsewhere." - Jailan Zayan, Egyptian writer.

Similar to Hofstede's cultural dimensions, this particular cultural framework is of Fons Trompenaars and Charles Hampden-Turner. In a nutshell, some people make decisions based on how they feel. Others use logic and reason. Some cultures do not reveal what they are thinking or feeling, display rather cool and self-possessed behavior, which is admired, and consider strong facial expressions or gestures as uncivilised and taboo. People with this description often come from 'neutral' cultures, such as England's.

In contrast, there are people who are fierier in nature, who display strong, expressive emotions, who reveal their thoughts and feelings and are rather transparent and who are less inhibited and more dramatic. People who fit this description are usually from 'emotional' cultures, such as Italy's or Egypt's.

Putting Things Into Perspective

So how does this translate into real life intercultural misunderstandings?

When my English mother moved to the Middle East to live with my Egyptian father, there were many things she had to learn. One summer, when my Egyptian cousins and siblings and I were all hanging out, my dear mother approached us to ask if we wanted to have burgers for dinner. "Yes!" we all chimed. My mum went around the group and took note of how many everybody wanted. When she came to my cousin, Hatem, he said: "None, thank you." My mother went away, made the specified number of burgers and returned with one or two for each person. Hatem, as ordered, got none.

A few evenings later, we were all playing at my grandmother's house and my mother approached us to see if we wanted burgers – again. The exact same thing happened. When she asked Hatem, he replied, "None, thank you."

A few days later, my father got a call from Hatem's mum. "It seems," she said on the phone to my father, "that Hatem thinks aunt Helen doesn't like him. Everytime she asks if people want burgers, they all get burgers and Hatem gets none."

My father paused.

"Did Hatem ask for any?" my father asked.

"No," came the reply. "He said he didn't want any."

My father cracked a smile and said: "Nadia, Helen is English. If Hatem says he doesn't want any, she won't make him any. What she says is what she means. Next time, tell Hatem to say 'yes!'

Needless to say, the next time my mum asked everyone if they wanted burgers, Hatem replied, "Yes! Three please!"

In the Egyptian culture, there is a lot of reading between the lines that occurs and if you are new to the game, you will not know this. My mother comes from England, where people are direct in their approaches and truth is highly valued. In Egypt, people will often decline an invitation for a drink or snack to show they are being polite so as not to put the host/hostess out. But the game in Egypt is as follows: you decline a few times, the host insists and even if you keep declining, they bring you a beverage anyway. Coming from her more direct culture, where directness is respected and seen as a sign of honesty and openness, my mother didn't know this and took what Hatem said at face value.

As mentioned, I grew up in a household where my parents were from polar-opposite cultures and there were many times I felt both conflicted and intrigued by this. For example, my father would always make sure I was home a certain time of night and that somebody respectable would drop me off because otherwise, "what would the security downstairs (at the bottom of our building) say?" Egyptians are very proud people and one's reputation is important. As a father of a house, you want to make sure your daughters carry a clean slate and have respectable names. This has a lot to do with saving face and being looked highly upon. As a child growing up, all I could think about was: Who cares what security think? We don't even know them!

Egyptians are very warm and hospitable people and, like the Greeks and Italians, they are happy to provide food for everyone and invite last minute guests to stay and eat. I always remember sitting at my grandmother's table with a ton of food in the middle and lots of people around it. In contrast, in England, I recall being at a friend's house when "tea-time" struck and I was told I had to go home. I was a little taken aback with this and talked to my mother who explained that in England this was the way things were. People cooked just enough to feed their families and no more. In Egypt, people cooked to feed the masses, and if there were leftovers, which there usually was, they would go to the helpers, drivers, cleaners. Food was never thrown away. This illustrates the stark contrast of an individualistic versus collective society where in one instance, the nucleus is valued and in the other, the group is prioritised.

I grew up in Kuwait but every summer my family and I would travel to both England and Egypt to visit with family. I was always amazed to see how differently our extended family greeted us. In Egypt, the family would practically suffocate us with hugs and kisses, demonstrating the warmth, affection and closeness in proximity Egyptians have. Family, both nucleus and extended, is the most important social network there is. My English family, on the other hand, would politely say hello, either wave or a brief kiss on the cheek and it felt as though we had just seen them yesterday. The English value personal space and usually maintain at least an arm's length in order to feel comfortable.

The English also greatly value personal privacy and will go to great lengths to protect it; whereas Egyptians feel it is important to share information amongst one another, whether it be in the family or at work. After all, according to Egyptians, how can decisions be made if not everyone knows what is going on?

It is examples like the ones above that got me interested in the intercultural topic and which lead me to study it further as a Masters of Arts in the UK. It was truly my life story and I wanted to investigate further. Why did one culture say 'black' and another say 'white'? Why did one culture say 'wrong', while the other called that very same thing 'right'? It didn't make sense to me, but I learnt very early on that there was no one 'right' way. There were many, many different ways. I am still shocked when I travel to places where people don't understand this, but I have been blessed to come from an intercultural background and have travelled and lived in over seven different countries on four continents.

Becoming Aware

"So what are you, then?" asked the student, exasperated.
   "I am awake," the Buddha replied. - Buddhist teaching

The solution to curbing intercultural misunderstandings starts with awareness. Simply being aware that other people do things differently and being open to that, is a mighty good start. People don't often intentionally want to be rude, but they do operate in the way they know how, which may be a different way to the way you operate. Instead of automatically reacting, take a step back and consider that there may be a difference in values in play. What one culture considers rude, another considers polite. What one culture considers beneficial, another deems futile. What one culture sees as annoying, another considers important.

If you're moving to new pastures, attending intercultural training workshops or events may be a great idea for you and your family to begin an effective integration process. Children can also benefit from this type of education and awareness as they will be going to schools and mixing with many peers who have alternative backgrounds.

The intercultural organisation known as SIETAR (Society for Intercultural Education Training and Research) is a great place to start looking if you want to find intercultural workshops and events near you that you'd like to attend. It exists globally: www.sietareu.org, www.sietarusa.org, www.sietaraustralasia.org/2019-conference, www.sietar-japan.org/, www.youngsietar.org, facebook.com/sietaruk/

If you are curious to read about my story further, my thesis, entitled 'Countering Culture Shock: An Intercultural Training Programme Tailored For Egyptian Sojourners in England' is available on Amazon and Barnes and Noble.

Bibliography

- Cornes, A. (2004) Culture From the Inside Out. Boston: Intercultural Press.
- Ferraro, G.P. (2002) The Cultural Dimension of International Business. New Jersey: Prentice Hall.
- Hofstede, G. & Hofstede, G.J. (2005) Cultures and Organizations: Software of the Mind (2nd Edition). New York: McGraw Hill.
- Storti, C. (1999) Figuring Foreigners Out. Maine: Intercultural Press.

- Trompenaars, F. & Hampden-Turner (1997) Riding the Waves of Culture: Understanding Cultural Diversity in Business (2nd Edition). London: Nicholas Brealey Publishing.
- Zayan, Jailan. (2007) Egypt: The culture smart guide to customs and etiquette. Cairo: The American University in Cairo Press.

The stories you should tell your multicultural kid every day

by Elisavet Arkolaki

"The most important thing that parents can do is talk and read to their children. During the toddler and preschool years, it is critical to provide children with different language and reading experiences." - G. Reid Lyon

There are so many studies and so much research all pointing to the direction that reading to our children from very early on, telling them stories, is paramount for their development. Literature and literacy are the direct product of a human need to understand the world through the simple act of telling stories. Humans have always been coming up with all sorts of stories, fables, and myths in order to better understand the people around them and make sense of the world. This is how the human race survived, lived, and evolved.

A brilliant way to help your multicultural children interiorize a strong sense of identity is by sharing traditional stories; the ones that span generations. Folklore stories and myths from their countries of origin keep the culture alive and help them connect with their roots, even when living outside the community. They can help them grow closer to their past and incorporate elements of tenderness and pride in their identity. Also, sharing stories from cultures that aren't their own can help them to better understand friends and classmates.

Then, there are these other stories, the ones you can recite yourself, and which can be told at the most diverse moments of the day and not just before bedtime. Use every opportunity you have to share with your child invented stories, heard stories, stories you've read together. I remember growing up listening to my father telling us three stories he had come up with himself, always the same, during our dinner time. This storytelling time was so special to us that we purposefully delayed finishing our food. We never got tired of them. These very same stories are now passed on to my children.

Books are also a powerful tool for our children, helping them to make sense of their homes, communities, the world at large. Literature provides their first window to a world beyond their five senses, a world that can be magically entered by the simple act of words and illustrations putting in motion the wheels of the internal mechanism called imagination. This is how they grow and this is how they develop into individuals who can think for themselves.

There are so many books out there to choose from and as parents, it is our responsibility to present to our young ones with fun stories accompanied by beautiful artwork that spark their curiosity and inspire them. For our multicultural children in particular, it can be very beneficial to pick up books with diverse characters with whom they can relate to. It is also advisable when the children start showing specific interests, to let them choose books on their own. One of our favorite family outings for instance is Saturday morning visits to the local library.

When it comes to which books are best, it's hard to give specific titles. Book preferences can be very subjective and I can only share with you which are our favorite ones right now. What I do know for a fact, is that the best books will grow with your child. Let's say you buy now 'Where am I from?' for your 5-year-old to read to him. If it becomes a favorite, at 6 he will be reciting the words to you and by 7 he will enjoy reading it on his own, all curled up somewhere cozy at home.

A good multicultural book should:

- present the character's culture accurately and sensitively;
- empower children of different ethnic backgrounds;
- have strong literary merit.

Here http://maltamum.com/the-best-picture-books-for-multicultural-children/ I have compiled a list of my personal favorite picture books for multicultural children.

A list of websites and blogs promoting multilingualism & multiculturalism

- Pactadopt.org features several important articles on the topics of adoption and race such as 'Dealing with racism - perspective of a white transracial adoptive parent' by Beth Hall, and 'Not just "white parents" with kids of color" - The importance of racial identity work for parents' by Dr. Gina Miranda Samuels
- https://multiculturalkidblogs.com/ is a supportive community which brings together parents, educators, bloggers, writers and artists from across the world. They work for understanding among people and oppose any kind of discrimination. Their mission is to inspire and support parents, caregivers and educators raising the next generation of global citizens.
- https://www.figt.org/ - Families in Global Transition is a welcoming forum for globally mobile individuals, families, and those working with them. They promote cross-sector connections for sharing research and developing best practices that support the growth, success and well-being of people crossing cultures around the world.
- https://www.thepiripirilexicon.com/ - Annabelle's background lies in linguistics. In particular applied linguistics, bilingualism and second language acquisition. She has a Master's degree and a Ph.D. in Bilingual Language Acquisition.
- https://kidworldcitizen.org/ - Becky is an ESL and Spanish teacher, mother of 5 bilingual and multicultural kids, who shares ideas to teach kids about world cultures and our planet through travel, food, music, celebrations, service, maps, art, and projects.
- http://andthenwemovedto.com/ - Mariam grew up in Bahrain, New York City and Karachi. As an adult, she has lived in the United States (Massachusetts and

Texas), United Kingdom, Germany, Pakistan, Denmark, Singapore and the United Arab Emirates. She's the writer of the book "This Messy Mobile Life: How a MOLA can help globally mobile families create a life by design."

- https://alldonemonkey.com - Leanna is a homeschooling mom to three who blogs about positive parenting, multicultural education, and spiritual education.
- http://www.expitterpattica.com/ - What's it like to be a global nomad? Read about Lucille's adventures as an expat mum raising a family on the move.
- https://bilingualkidspot.com/ - Raising Bilingual or Multilingual Kids
- Raisingworldchildren.com - A collaborative online and in print publication that talks about empowering children to thrive in a Multicultural world. Simple strategies or new perspectives to challenges otherwise less spoken about provided in every article from a different voice.
- http://iamatriangle.com/triangle-story/ - Read the triangle story here: "Imagine a place called Circle Country. Everyone who lives inside of its borders are Circle Citizens. The Circle Country has very specific culture, holidays, celebrations, food preferences, a language that is unique to them as well as music, education and political categories. Let's also talk about Square Society. Everyone who lives inside of its borders are Square Settlers. The Square Society also has the culture, holidays, celebrations, food preferences (and on and on) as the Circle Country, but they are completely different..."
- https://multiculturalchildrensbookday.com/ - Their mission is to not only raise awareness for the kid's books that celebrate diversity, but to get more of these books into classrooms and libraries.
- Creativeworldofvarya.com - A blog for parents raising Multicultural and Multilingual children. Here you can find craft, parenting advice, tips on having a baby in China, our adventures as a family of five, book reviews and more.
- Kidsspanishbookclub.blogspot.com - Aims to establish awareness of books mainly for younger kids that can help them and their parents in practicing their Spanish from an early age.
- KidsTravelBooks.com - Aims to encourage families to learn about other cultures through travel and books.

- www.growingupgupta.com - A multicultural lifestyle blog that is dedicated to openly discussing interracial/intercultural dating and marriage, multicultural parenting, fusion recipes, and more.
- https://www.letthejourneybegin.eu/ - Tells the story of a trilingual, multicultural family. From the bio: "It's about the journey of parenting while navigating different languages and cultures. About the beauty and difficulty of living abroad, and about raising little world citizens through language, travel, and food."
- www.themultilingualhome.com -The blogger shares their family's love of languages and adventures through home school, language learning, recipes, religion, travel, multicultural and expat experiences. They have 3 kids and speak 6 languages between them.
- www.globetrottinkids.com - Features books and resources for global education in the elementary classroom.
- http://discoveringtheworldthroughmysonseyes.com/ - France's blog is the story of her family's life, a multicultural family living, learning and discovering the world through their son's eyes. She writes about bilingualism, multicultural books, food (recipes), crafts, traditions, and more.
- www.joysunbear.com - This website features stories to teach kids about diverse cultures around the world; included, videos and blogs on social-emotional learning, crafts, coloring pages, recipes. The aim is to empower kids to love and respect themselves and others by learning about diversity and unity.
- https://chalkacademy.com/ - Betty writes about raising trilingual children and relearning Chinese with them in a non-diverse American town. Lots of teaching tips, crafts, free printables, book reviews, music, and educational video recs. Her mission is to make bilingual resources more accessible and provide encouragement to all families.
- https://kidsspanishbookclub.blogspot.com/ - Adee grew up in a household where they spoke only English, and her first exposure to a foreign language was to Spanish in seventh grade. She obtained a minor in Spanish at the City College of NY (CUNY), she took a semester of Mandarin Chinese and night classes in Italian, as herself is of Italian and Irish ancestry. Her hope is to expose the young ones to the beauty of the Spanish language through the joy of reading.

- https://www.BiculturalMama.com - This site covers parenting and culture from the perspective of a bicultural family (Asian/White). Content has a heavier focus on Asian culture as that is the blogger's background. Parenting topics lean more heavily towards younger children like preschoolers and elementary school kids. She also covers healthy living, food, and a bit of travel that relate to families.

- www.ketchupmoms.com - They mainly cover travel with kids, books and movies for kids, food recipes and positive female role models.

- www.MissPandaChinese.com - Amanda shares the Chinese language and world culture with parents and educators on her blog.

- https://polyglotparenting.com/ - Ilana Shydlo's expertise in bilingualism stems from her background in Speech-Language Pathology. Lots of informational articles on her blog.

- http://growingupglobal.net/ - Homa Tavangar is the author of "Growing Up Global: Raising Children to Be At Home in the World", one of the first resources published to help parents raise children as global citizens. She advises children's media, schools and other organizations on global citizenship, empathy, equity, diversity and inclusion; is an active volunteer and mother of three daughters.

- http://bilingualmonkeys.com/ - Bilingual Monkeys offers strategies and support for busy parents seeking to raise bilingual children. This site, created by an educator and parent who has worked with hundreds of bilingual and multilingual children for over 20 years, provides practical ideas and inspiration to help meet this challenge with greater success—and experience greater joy in the process.

- https://www.mamasmiles.com/ - MaryAnne was raised in the United States, Guatemala, France, Bolivia, and Austria. Her first daughter was born in Scotland, and she now lives with her husband and their four children in Silicon Valley, California. She writes about parenting, crafts, and education.

- http://acraftyarab.com/ - Kay Tarapolsi is a Libyan American who creates art to promote a positive image of Arab and Islamic culture.

- https://littlenomadas.com/ - Flor is a Venezuelan-American former attorney and certified language and intercultural trainer currently living in Germany. She started her expat journey about two decades ago when she married her American sweetheart and moved to the United States where they started a beautiful family.

- https://www.incultureparent.com/ is an online magazine for parents raising little global citizens. Centered around culture, tradition and language, they feature articles on parenting around the world and raising multicultural and multilingual (also bicultural and bilingual) children.
- http://mylittleoneandme-debolina-raja-gupta.blogspot.com/ - Indian Mommy Blogger and her journey with her two girls. The joys, experiences, frustrations and rewards of being a mommy.
- https://www.expat.com/ - Provides free information and advice to expats and expats-to-be, by inviting them to share their experience. Their goal is to help all those living or wishing to live overseas and everybody can participate.
- http://www.mixedremixed.org/ - Established in 2013 (USA), the Mixed Remixed Festival brings together film and book lovers, innovative and emerging artists, and multiracial families and individuals, Hapas, and families of transracial adoption for workshops, readings, film screenings and live performance including music, comedy and spoken word.
- http://www.thelogonauts.com/ - A resource for diverse and global books for middle to upper elementary.
- https://www.multilingualcafe.com/ - Bilingual blog, French and English. Their mission is the transmission of languages and cultures in bilingual / multilingual / multicultural families and the promotion of plurilingualism and multiculturalism.
- Language Magazine https://www.languagemagazine.com/ - Monthly publication that provides cutting-edge information for language learners, educators, and professionals around the world.
- https://tandemnomads.com/ - Amel comes from Algeria, she became Austrian by marriage, she was born in India and lived as a child and as an adult in 8 countries and 13 cities. She's very passionate about topics related to innovative businesses and social entrepreneurship.

- https://sundaebean.com/page/15/?cat=-1 - Expat Happy Hour, rated #1 podcast episode on iTunes Places & Travel. Sundae Bean is an intercultural strategist. She's an American by birth, Swiss by marriage, expat in South Africa by choice.
- Makingherehome.com - Expat life, family life abroad, travel, and The Expat Book Club.
- https://xpatarchive.com/ - The Expatriate Archive Centre (non-profit) collects and preserves the life stories of expatriates worldwide for future research. They are located in The Netherlands but their outreach is global. They are here to serve researchers around the world.
- Expat.com - It is the largest expat social network. Whether you are about to relocate or already living in your host country, expat.com helps you throughout your project.
- https://thinkingnomads.com/ - Discussing and exploring alternative ways to live and work while on the road.
- https://blog.languagelizard.com/ - Supporting Multicultural Classrooms & Bilingual Families. Resources for Teachers and Parents.

My Notes

Printed in Great Britain
by Amazon